THE DOCTRINE
OF
SOVEREIGN GRACE

Opened and Vindicated
from Holy Scripture

ISAAC BACKUS

SOLID GROUND CHRISTIAN BOOKS
BIRMINGHAM, ALABAMA USA

OTHER SOLID GROUND TITLES

We recently celebrated our eighth anniversary of uncovering buried treasure to the glory of God. During these eight years we have produced over 225 volumes. A sample is listed below:

Biblical & Theological Studies: *Addresses to Commemorate the 100th Anniversary of Princeton Theological Seminary in 1912* by Allis, Machen, Wilson, Vos, Warfield etc.

Notes on Galatians by J. Gresham Machen

The Origin of Paul's Religion by J. Gresham Machen

A Scientific Investigation of the Old Testament by R.D. Wilson

Theology on Fire: *Sermons from Joseph A. Alexander*

Evangelical Truth: *Sermons for the Family* by Archibald Alexander

A Shepherd's Heart: *Pastoral Sermons of James W. Alexander*

Grace & Glory: *Sermons from Princeton Chapel* by Geerhardus Vos

The Lord of Glory by Benjamin B. Warfield

The Person & Work of the Holy Spirit by Benjamin B. Warfield

The Power of God unto Salvation by Benjamin B. Warfield

Calvin Memorial Addresses by Warfield, Johnson, Orr, Webb…

The Five Points of Calvinism by Robert Lewis Dabney

Annals of the American Presbyterian Pulpit by W.B. Sprague

The Word & Prayer: *Classic Devotions from the Pen of John Calvin*

A Body of Divinity: *Sum and Substance of Christian Doctrine* by Ussher

The Complete Works of Thomas Manton (in 22 volumes)

A Puritan New Testament Commentary by John Trapp

Exposition of the Epistle to the Hebrews by William Gouge

Exposition of the Epistle of Jude by William Jenkyn

Lectures on the Book of Esther by Thomas M'Crie

Lectures on the Book of Acts by John Dick

To order any of our titles please contact us in one of three ways:

Call us at **1-866-789-7423**

Email us at **sgcb@charter.net**

Visit our website at **www.solid-ground-books.com**

THE
DOCTRINE
OF
SOVEREIGN GRACE

Opened and Vindicated
From Holy Scripture

And Also

The Consistency and Duty of Declaring Divine Sovereignty,
And Men's Impotency, while yet we Address Their Consciences
With the Warnings of Truth, and Calls of the Gospel.

By Isaac Backus
Pastor of a Church in Middleborough

*"I am not ashamed of the Gospel of Christ;
for it is the Power of God unto Salvation,
to everyone that believeth."* – Romans 1:16

PROVIDENCE, Rhode-Island
Printed by JOHN CARTER

Solid Ground Christian Books
PO Box 660132
Vestavia Hills AL 35266
205-443-0311
sgcb@charter.net
solid-ground-books.com

The Doctrine of Sovereign Grace Opened and Vindicated
by Isaac Backus (1724-1806)

First Solid Ground Edition June 2009

Taken from the edition published by
The Predestinarian Publisher
1159 County Road 420
Quitman, MS 39355

Cover design by Borgo Design, Tuscaloosa, AL

Cover image from Ric Ergenbright.
View his images at **ricergenbright.com**

ISBN: 978-159925-208-7

TABLE OF CONTENTS

THE

DOCTRINE

OF

SOVEREIGN GRACE

Opened and Vindicated.

P A R T---I

The chief occasion of the ensuing discourse is this: About four years ago, on a view of the prevailing disposition in multitudes, either to pry into futurities, to the neglect of present duty, or to contend about religion, instead of regarding the life and practice of it, while the vanities of time carried the world before them, I was moved to publish a discourse from James 2:22, with this title, *True Faith Will Produce Good Works*. And through the whole endeavoured to handle the glorious truths of the gospel in a practical way; and had as little expectation of being publicly attacked therefor as for any thing I ever wrote: And I was not alone in this thought, for a worthy minister in *Great Britain* says, in a letter, "Your sermon on the Fruits of Faith is well adapted to silence gainsayers." Yet how often are we disappointed in this evil world!

Mr. *Daniel Martin,* Elder of a Baptist Church in *Rehoboth,* published a piece last fall, entitled, *Some Meditations on the Plain Testimony of the Holy Scriptures, relating to the elect or chosen* of God, etc., wherein, after inserting as a motto our Saviour's caution to take heed how and what we hear he begins thus: "Having received the foregoing caution and instruction from the most wonderful Counsellor that ever spoke on earth, I have made the following observations on several points of doctrine delivered by Mr. *Isaac Backus,* in his book entitled, *True Faith Will Produce Good Works,* wherein he has made many worthy observations, and given divers good instructions; but to my sorrow he has *advanced several points of doctrine, which appear to me to be in opposition to the sense and pure meaning of the holy scriptures."* And he goes on to bend all his force through his whole performance against the peculiar doctrines of sovereign grace.

Several reasons were suggested, in my own mind and by others, against making any reply to this piece at all: As that it is so plainly erroneous, that it was not likely to do much hurt; that there is no end of controversy; and it is peculiarly disagreeable for one Baptist to contend with another, who have so many others against them on every side. But in answer to this, it appears, that as plain as these errors are, yet many are carried away with them; and though contention is disagreeable, yet if we can see *"the faith once delivered to the saints"* betrayed, and hold our peace, how shall we answer it to him who has required us to contend *earnestly* there-for? And will not a just view of the last objection turn its weight the other way? For an engine which has been much used, both in past and present age, to prejudice people against the Baptists, has been to represent them as unsound in gospel doctrine; and now when an aged elder of that denomination has represented to the world, that to hold, "That faith is not of man," carries in it that "He that is justified by faith, is justified because God has given it to him; and he that believes not is damned, because God has not given him faith;" p. 15, if we let such reproaches against sovereign grace pass unanswered, because in our denomination, what a handle would others make of it, to represent us all either as corrupt in principle, or else more after party than truth? Nay, if those who met their *enemies* ox or ass going astray, and did not bring it back again, broke a command of God, Exodus 23:4; how can we answer it to Him, if we see our *friends* and fellow mortals going in a way that we are fully convinced leads to destruction, and not attempt, as we have opportunity, to show them their danger? *Paul's* earnest desire for the salvation of his brethren and kinsfolk, moved him to take pains to convince them, that, though they followed after the law of righteousness, yet that they did quite miss their way, because they sought it *not by faith, but as it were by the deeds of the law*. Rom. 9:22. And as it appears to me that Mr. Martin has missed the right way in the same respect, I think it a duty to attempt in a brief and plain manner to show him wherein he has done so.

The grand point which he objects to in my book, is the manner of my holding *election:* He professes to hold it; but thinks I hold it in a wrong way. I had observed from Eph. 1:3-7, that *Paul* says; *"He has chosen us, that we should be holy"*; but the modern notions are, that he chooses us because *we are holy*, making that to be the *cause*, which *Paul* viewed to be the *effect:* All the controversy turns upon this point, whether the good pleasure of God's will, or our *free will*, be the cause of our holiness and happiness. Mr. *Martin* mentions this, and answers, that *both* are the cause thereof, p. 6. To prove which, he cites many declarations of God's good will, and then says, "Since it is the good will of God that all men should be saved and come to the knowledge of the truth, what does hinder, or indeed what can hinder or prevent, but the want of man's good will?" p. 7. Aye, sure enough, what else can hinder? But since that is *wanting*, how can it be any cause of our salvation? *Solomon* says; "that which is wanting cannot be numbered" (Ecc. 1:15). Yet behold! Here is one *"wiser than Solomon"*! For he can reckon that which is *wanting* for a principal part of the capital sum! Perhaps it will be said, if it is wanting in one, it may not in another. This I suppose is the thing aimed at, for he says, "By free will I understand good will; when, a man's will is to do the will of God." p. 7. And again, "We may assure ourselves, that God has not hid the light of the gospel from any man or people, who desire and seek after the knowledge of God." p. 13. Who pretends that He does? I was so far from doing of it, that in answer to an objection, p. 82, I observed, that "We may be heartily willing to do many outward actions, which yet we cannot do, and so are excused from blame in our not doing them; but the cause why souls cannot believe the record which God has given of His Son; and love and obey Him with all their hearts, is because they *love darkness rather than light; yea, hate the light,* because the *carnal mind is enmity against God.*" (John 3:19-20; Rom. 8:7). And if our advocate for free will and good works read this and much more to the same purpose in my book, before he wrote against it, where are his good works, while he misrepresents my sentiments? And if he did not read it, where is his regard to equity, to condemn a man without a hearing?

Mr. *Martin* has told us, that by free will he understands a will to do the will of God; but he has not informed us who the people are, or where they live, that naturally have such a will: He is not so fair in this respect, as *Robert Barclay* was about *perfection*; for though he labored much to prove that such a state was attainable in this life; yet he says, "With respect to myself, I speak modestly, because I ingeniously confess that I have not yet attained it (NOTE: By the way I would here observe, that as in my late *Plea for Liberty of Conscience*, I happened to mention it as a *Quaker* notion, that when a person has the Spirit with him, he is then perfect; I would now retract that sentence; for I am informed by a principal leader among them, that I mistook their sentiments, and that I would always watch against misrepresenting any people, though I differ ever so much from them. He informs me that they hold sanctification to be a progressive work, and that a person may be under powerful influences of the Spirit, and yet have remaining corruptions, though they suppose that a perfect victory over them is attainable in this life. Now as I willingly retract my mistake of their sentiments, so I think it but a friendly part to let them know, that for friend *Barclay*, in p. 8, of his Apology, to represent that "Those who plead for justification wholly by the imputation of a righteousness without them, deny the necessity of being clothed with an inward righteousness," is not just; for no men upon earth hold stronger to the necessity of regeneration and inward sanctification, than those who trust alone on Christ's imputed righteousness for their justification before God.)."

So, here I believe every one of *Adam's children,* who are brought to a true sight of their case, will concur with the Apostle's confession, that *"all have sinned and come short of the glory of God"*; and that *all* go on, either secretly or openly, to serve divers lusts and pleasures, till the kindness and love of God our Saviour appears, *"not by works of righteousness which we have done, but according to His mercy,* to save us, by the *washing of regeneration, and renewing of the Holy Ghost"* (Rom. 3:23; Tit. 3:3-5). Our author's notion that both God's will and ours are the cause of our salvation, runs him into the following absurdities:

First, To exclude all those divine testimonies which prove man's universal depravity: that both *Jews* and *Gentiles* are all under sin, and there is *none* righteous, no *not one*; are *all* gone out of the way, and *none* that doth good, no *not one*; that we are *by nature* children of wrath, *even as others*; that the Scripture hath concluded all under sin (Rom. 3:9-19; Eph. 2:3; Gal. 3:22). I say his notion excludes all such testimonies of truth, of which the Bible is full, even so far, that though his book is filled with texts which he imagines will prove universal redemption, yet I think he never takes notice of one that proves our universal depravity, notwithstanding he talks much of keeping close to Scripture.

Second, As the nature of his scheme is the same as that which ensnared the *Galatians*, so it is attended with the same consequence which the Apostle mentions to them: It would *frustrate* the grace of God, and make Christ to *die in vain* (Gal. 2:21). For if men have a will to do the will of God, they had no need of a Saviour to die for them, and if they have it not, they are like to perish, notwithstanding what He has done; for Mr. *Martin* says, "It seems by our Lord's parable (Luke 14:16-20), that there was nothing wanting on the part of him that made the supper, but on the part of them that were bidden; their good will was lacking;

their will and affections were on earthly things." p. 7. Therefore by his scheme, unless our Lord could find some of the children of men who had not their will and affections on earthly things, His great Supper will be lost: Nay it must unavoidably be so; for if any could be found with such a good will as our author describes, the Saviour could have no right to call them to this Supper, because *"He came not to call the righteous, but sinners to repentance"* (Luke 5:32). Then turn which way you will, this notion of free will *frustrates* the grace of God, and would make Christ to *die in vain*. Mr. *Martin* says, "They did not improve the power He had given them." I know they did not improve it right, for they improved it to excuse themselves from coming, and to pursue their own ways. Again he asserts, that "Faith is work which God requireth of man, and what our Lord taught the people to labor in." p. 14. And to prove it refers us to John 6:27-29. Though in this he discovers a darker notion about faith than the *Jews* did, for it appears that they knew that faith is giving credit to another, and not a work of our own; therefore in the next words they ask for a sign, that they might see and believe, and they plainly intimate, that though he had fed five thousand, yet *Moses* had done much more, even fed six hundred thousand of their fathers in the wilderness, so that they were not inclined to leave *Moses for Jesus*; and though he assured them that it was not *Moses* who gave that bread, and that the Father had now given the true bread from heaven, yet their disposition and conduct discovered plainly, that it must be the *work of God* to make any of them believe it. Mr. *Martin* is so far from allowing this point, that he ventures to declare, that "The unbeliever is not made a believer by the mighty power of God working in him, but by hearing and receiving the word." p. 30. And so because the word is the instrument of faith, he denies that God by His power is the *author* of it; and holds it to be "of man." p. 14. Hence,

Third, His plan would make the will of the Creator *dependent* on the will of the creature; for he labors much to prove that full provision is made for the salvation of all men, while he owns that many miss of it, because their good will is wanting, yet denies the exertion of divine power to work faith in any; the certain consequence of which is, that it *depends* upon man's will whether God shall ever have his good will in the salvation of one soul or not. This consequence is so unanswerable, that it seems our author dare not meddle with it; for I had mentioned it in a quotation from one of our Baptist elders in *Carolina,* at the foot of my 56th page; yet though he quotes a passage out of the middle of that page, he never says a word upon this glaring absurdity which attends his doctrine. For the reader's satisfaction, I will give him the passage I quoted. It is this: "*Conditional election* sets up an *inferior* cause above a *superior*; making election and salvation no more than a *may be*, instead of a *shall be*. It represents the Almighty as ever fluctuating in His councils, taking up with new consultations *dependent* on the fickle will of man, and the uncertain acts that flow there-from; by which method He is brought in saying, "0! I will if they will, and O! that they may will to believe, become holy, diligently and perseveringly improving their flock of free will abilities, that they may be saved; never the less NOT MY WILL, but THEIR WILL be done (NOTE: Mr. *Isaac Chandler's* Doctrines of Grace, printed at *Boston*, 1744, p. 208.)!" Now since this lay directly in Mr. *Martin's* way, what reason can be given for his avoiding any mention of it, but because he could not answer it? I confess it is beyond my weak capacity to conceive how it can be fairly answered, and if others can, it would certainly be much more to the purpose to do it, than what they on that side generally dwell upon. The sum of all our author's meditations is, he imagines that to hold the good pleasure of God's will to be the sole cause of our salvation, and that faith is His gift, and wrought in these by His own power would carry this dreadful consequence in it, 'That men cannot be judged and rewarded according to their works, but according as He hath given, or neglected to give.' And he seems as much affrighted at this imagination as over a timorous person was at a black stump in the night: He has it over and over from one end of his pamphlet to the other, and upon every mention of it, he turns away to a number of Scriptures, which prove that God is both just and merciful, which we hold as fully as he does; also upon every view of my pleas for God's sovereignty and power, that frightful image rises in view again, which makes such powerful impressions upon him, that he seems not to know Scripture when he runs against it. For instance, I had observed, p. 33, that saving faith is a receiving with all the heart the witness and testimony that God has given of eternal life in his Son, and he who believeth not hath made him a liar (1st John 5:9-12), the evidence of which truth shines so clear as to leave all without excuse, who do not believe with all their hearts; while every soul that is made willing by divine power to receive His testimony, and set to his seal that God is true, knows that this *"faith is not of himself, it is the gift of God"*. I thus marked these last words as Scripture, and in the margin referred to the text, (Eph. 2:8), yet Mr. *Martin*, after citing this passage, says, "Is it right to say, because faith is the gift of God, that therefore it is not of man?" And after bringing many texts to try to prove that this is not true, he says, "Now let us consider a little of the consequence of this *vain notion*, that faith is not *of man."* p. 14, *15.* And so recurs to his frightful imagination again, without being sensible that he is not here contending with *Isaac Backus* but with divine revelation. And I must confess that those who hold to his doctrine of free will, would be more consistent to own themselves *Deists,* than to act as they now do; for Dr. *Young,* the most open Deist that I have heard of in this country, published a piece in his own defense, in the *Boston Evening-Post,* the 27th of last *August,* wherein he declares, he has as great a veneration for many glorious things in the Old and New Testaments as any Christian in this country; but says, there are some things in the Scriptures that he does not understand. And what are they? Why says he, "Such as how God can be said to predestinate one to everlasting life, and leave another to inevitable and eternal perdition, and yet *of a truth*, be no respecter of persons." This he thinks to be inconsistent, and therefore rejects those parts of Scripture that teach it: Mr. *Martin* professes to hold all the Scripture, and yet the center of all his difficulty with me, is exactly the same that the Deist has against the Bible, because it teaches that doctrine. And the bottom of the matter with both is, because they think they *deserve* something better than to be left to perish in their sins: For if that were not the case, any person of common sense can easily see the right the *householder* had to *give* to some what they did not deserve, while he did not fail to let every one have their due; and can see the iniquity of those who *murmured* at the *good man* for so doing. Yea vulgar understandings can easily comprehend the justice of that striking demand, *"Is it not lawful for me to do what I will with mine own? Is thine eye evil because I am good?"* Our Lord tells us that the kingdom of heaven is *like* this. (*Matt. 20:1-15*). Therefore,

Fourth, This scheme would rob God of his essential *glory.* I had observed, that the respect of persons which is condemned in Scripture, is a *perverting of justice,* and every pious soul detests such a thought concerning the Godhead;

yet we have early notice of His respecting persons in another sense, for He had *respect* to *Abel* and to his offering; but unto *Cain* and to his offering He had not *respect;* which made *Cain very wroth.* And I observed that God's demand on him upon that occasion was as much as if He had said, 'Do you think I am so unjust, as not to accept all that is well done?" Mr. *Martin* takes notice, that I acknowledge that well-doing is accepted, and yet, as if I had disowned it, he goes on and brings many texts which prove that saints will be rewarded in the great day, and then says, "I think it is plain, that for any to hold that God, without any just cause arising from what He foresaw in one man more than another, has chosen or elected a particular number to salvation, and left all the rest to perish in their sins, is unjust and unequal." p. 5, 6. This is the man who has often cautioned his readers against the *slight* of men, and *craft* of deceivers; but what shall we call his conduct here? He heaps up texts, which, the reader may think he has proved his point well, and of course that his antagonist is very erroneous; but what has he proved? Why he has proved that saints will be rewarded, and who has ever denied it? He knows I did not, yet he will have it that there was something foreseen in them better than others, which was the cause of their being chosen and saved: It is in plain terms as much as to say, 'It is unjust and unequal for God to *give* salvation to some sinners, and leave the rest to perish, unless He saw that some *deserved* salvation more than others;' which would make election and salvation to be of *debt,* and not of *grace,* contrary to the whole Bible.

For this writer to hold, that because God will reward the *righteous,* that therefore it would be unequal for Him to choose some *sinners* to life, without seeing any good in them more than others, while He left the rest to perish, is as unreasonable as it would be to argue, that a Nobleman could not justly bestow a *free favor* upon any undeserving person, because he must *pay* his workmen their due; or to say, because the King must execute *justice,* that therefore he has no right to show *mercy!* And to represent, that holding saving faith to be not of ourselves, but the gift of God; implies, that He must "Judge and condemn some poor sinful men to eternal destruction for His own neglect," p. 15, is as false as to say, because the King pardons some criminals, therefore the rest are executed for his neglect! When, in truth the latter are executed for their crimes, while the others are saved by the King's mercy; a just view whereof will move them to love and obey him all their days; to illustrate which was the main design of my book, yet our advocate for justice and equity has picked out a few sentences, without regarding the connection of the discourse, and exerted all his wit to cloth my doctrine with the most blasphemous garment he has mentioned above! If such treatment of our Creator and fellow-creatures, is the natural effect of this notion of free will instead of free grace, what cause have we to abhor, and bear testimony against it!

I had remarked, that Jesus was so far from giving foreseen faith and good works as the cause of babes receiving gospel grace, instead of the wise and prudent, that He resolves it into the Father's pleasure alone, *"for so it seemed good in thy sight"*(Matt. 11:26). Mr. Martin cites this passage, p. 9, and then fills up four pages with Scriptures and reasoning, to prove that grace is proclaimed to all, and that those who perish will be justly condemned, and reckons it strange that I or any man should think, "That God did not foresee that when this grace appeared to all men, some would believe and obey; or if it be concluded that He did, that He should have no regard thereunto in His choice." But what a slight of man is here? I asserted the two first of these points as plainly as he has, and hold them as fully, yet by this method he insinuates the contrary. I also hold as strongly as he can, that God foresaw that a number would believe and obey; but the grand point between us is, *how* they come to do it? He says, men's living in sin and not turning to the Lord is the cause of their destruction, and if men turn they shall live, p. 11. I say the same with all my heart; but still the question between us is not answered, which is, *how they came to turn*? How unfair is it in disputing for the opponent to deny a proposition, and then run round and prove several other things, which the respondent holds as much as he does, and then boast of gaining the argument, without ever touching the point in debate? I had proved that Jesus resolved the cause of babes receiving the gospel, into the Father's pleasure alone: My opponent denies it, and then brings many proofs that the wicked's destruction will be just, and that those who turn shall live, without the least evidence that any of *Adam's* race have any free will power to turn themselves, or that God had any regard to such a power in choosing one rather than another, which is the very matter in dispute. I dare say, if Mr. *Martin* should assert, that none but believers are the proper subjects of baptism under the gospel, and one should deny it, and then produce many proofs that children were circumcised under the law, which he knows as well as they, he would hardly allow that he was fairly confuted; yet that would be full as fair as his treatment of me here.

And what shall we say, if to unfairness men border hard upon untruths? He says, "To prove this scheme, Mr. *Backus* has brought out of the whole Bible *one* text, which is Matt. 11:26," p. 12, as if that one text was all I had produced to prove that grace is bestowed in a way of entire sovereignty; when in the very page before, I brought Luke 4:15-29, where it appears that the inhabitants of *Nazareth* attended with admiration to what Jesus preached concerning *grace*, as long as they imagined that they had a better claim thereto than others. But when He let them know, from the instance of favor shown to a widow among the *Sidonians*, and to a leper among the *Syrians*, which favor was not shown to any in *Israel*; that He had as good right to

Give salvation to the *heathen,* and to leave the Jews to perish in their sins;---then those who wondered at his *gracious words* before, were *filled with wrath,* and rose up and THRUST him out. I say I had quoted this Scripture in the foregoing page, with a larger comment upon it than I have given now, to prove the absolute sovereignty of grace; yet Mr. *Martin* skips over it without any notice, and would have the reader believe that I could bring but one text to favor my plan in all the Bible.

Sovereignty God claims as his peculiar glory, therefore in answer to the earnest request of *Moses* for a sight of his *glory,* He says, *"I will be gracious to whom I will be gracious, and will shew mercy to whom I will shew mercy"* (Exod. 33:19). And the Apostle Paul cites this passage, and then concludes thus upon it: *"So then it is NOT OF him that willeth, NOR OF him that runneth, but OF GOD that sheweth mercy"* (Rom. 9:16). But our late reasoner says, "Most certainly BOTH the good will of God and the *free will of man* is the *cause* of their holiness and happiness," p. 6. I leave it to the reader's consideration, which of them is to be credited, and proceed to observe, that as this scheme would rob God of his glory, so,

Five, It would *cheat men of their souls,* by flattering them along in false hopes till they sink in despair. I know my opponent calls it a *dark and discouraging* scheme to hold that God hath chosen only a particular number to salvation, and that without any regard to their faith and obedience, p. 12. But let the matter be well examined: We both profess that full provision is made in the gospel for the salvation of sinners, and I believe that God will *make His people willing* in the day of *His power* (Psalm 110:5), to serve Him in the *beauty of holiness;* that all who are given by the Father to the Son, *shall come to Him;* and that *no man can come except the Father draw him,* which drawing is by the *teaching* and almighty influence of the Holy Ghost (*Psalm* 110:3; John 6:37, 44, 45, 63 and 16:8). But Mr. *Martin* holds, that though God's good will has made provision for us, yet that it must be *of our* free will, *of our* good will, if we ever come to partake of it, p. 6, 7. Therefore as long as souls conceit they have or can work up such a good will, they go on with self-righteous hopes; but when they find that they have not such a free will power, and cannot work it up, they must sink in despair, not withstanding the help this scheme can afford them. He calls it a *bold assertion* for me to say, faith is wrought in the soul by the exceeding greatness of divine power; and says, for this I quote but one text, viz. Eph. 1:19, p. 27, which is not true, for in the same sentence (p. 31 of my book) I quote another which calls Jesus the *author* and *finisher of faith,* Heb. 12:2. And though he imagines that the power spoken of in Eph. 1:19, is only what is exerted to assist the believer in doing wonders, and not a "Power which none can hinder, working faith in them who have not believed", p. 27, and presumes to say, "The unbeliever is not made a believer by the mighty power of God working in him," p. 30. Yet alas! what an awful case should we be in, if this was all the hope that the gospel gave! The *letter killeth*, but the *Spirit giveth life*. The *veil* will remain upon our hearts, till the Spirit of the Lord takes it away, and gives us with open face to behold the divine glory, by which we are *changed* into the same image, 2nd Cor. 3:6-18. And since Mr. *Martin* denies that the power spoken of in Eph. 1:19, which raised Christ from the dead, is the power that first makes a sinner a believer, I would desire him to read on to the next chapter, where truth says, *"When we were dead in sins God hath quickened us together with Christ:--- By grace are ye saved, through faith; and that NOT OF yourselves: It is the gift of God; not of works, lest any man should boast, for we are his workmanship, CREATED in Christ Jesus unto good works"*. And if he will dare to say, that *creating* power, and the power that *quickens the dead*, is not the power that "none can hinder", I shall not think it worth while for any man to reason farther with him; but hoping that he will not resist the light to such a degree, I would request him to review the absurdity of his notion, that a greater power is displayed to assist the believer than to convert a sinner; that is, that a greater power is exerted to help Christ's friends, than to conquer his enemies! (Read Psalm 45:1-7, compared with Heb. 1:8-9).

Thus I have shown, that the notion of persons being elected because of their foreseen faith and obedience, and that God has made full provision for all, yet does not exert His power to bring any to embrace it, but leaves that to the creatures' will, excludes all the abundant testimony that truth has given to man's universal depravity, would frustrate the grace of God, and make Christ to die in vain; would make the will of the Creator dependent on that of the creature, and rob God of his essential glory, while it would embolden worms to glory in His presence, that they were better than others, till they sink in discouragement and despair, by finding their imaginary excellency and power fail them. But on the other hand, that to hold forth the free proclamation of the gospel to the *chief of sinners*, and that Christ died for the *ungodly*, and has given the Spirit to convince and *change* their souls, working *in them* all the good pleasure of his goodness, and the *work of faith with power* (2nd Thes. 1:11), opens a glorious door of hope to guilty sinners, and gives courage to the believer to strive according to his working, *"who worketh in him mightily"* (Col. 1:29).

Mr. *Martin*, in order to make out that though faith is the gift of God, yet that it is *of man*, says, "Our temporal food and raiment are the gifts of God, are they therefore not of men? Hath not God ordained that man should get bread by the sweat of his face? Gen. 3:19-23. And when He fed his people, *Israel*, with bread from heaven, and quails in the wilderness, they had it together, and dressed, and did not eat thereof without their labor; so then faith being the gift of

God, does not hinder its being the work and labor of men," p. 14. Upon which I would remark,

1. That here is no distinction made between natural and spiritual actions, between which there is as great a difference as there is between soul and body. We all grant that men have a natural power to do *rational* actions, but the question is, whether any have ability to perform any spiritual or holy action, before they are regenerated by the Holy Spirit or not?

2. It is the divine appointment that our temporal food and raiment should be raised out of the earth by our labor, but to hold salvation upon such a footing, would make it of *works* and; not of *grace;* contrary to the whole gospel.

3. We allow that the manna that was rained round the *Israelite's tents,* was a type of the heavenly food which is brought near to our souls in the gospel, and as they were to receive and eat of it freely, so the gospel calls us to a feast where *all things are now ready;* but how ridiculous would a messenger appear, that should come and call the poor and needy to a *free* entertainment, upon condition they will first *work hard for it!* None expect that persons will enjoy the benefit of food, though ever so choice and free, if they do not receive it; but who ever thought that eating food was working for it, or performing a condition to obtain it? However, as coming and eating imply local motion and bodily exercise, we are in danger of having our minds somewhat darkened by this similitude, if we do not correct it

by others; therefore our Lord, in his discourse to *Nicodemus,* compares believing to *Israel's* looking to the brazen serpent, which was not a local motion nor long exercise; but as quick as sight; neither had they any thing to recommend them, for they were poisoned in a deadly manner, and that as the fruit of their sin; but they were called to look off from themselves to the remedy which God had freely provided, and as many as did so received immediate healing. So do all those who behold the Lamb of God that taketh away the sin of the world. The very notion of faith carries us off from ourselves, for it is admitting the testimony of another, and not any work of ours; our character has no concern in the affair, as whether we are poor or rich, worthy or unworthy, for it depends entirely upon the evidence that we have of the credibility of the speaker; And though we often strive against, or try to avoid the light, because our deeds are evil, yet when our souls are brought to receive divine truth, it is no more of our work than it is to see and enjoy the light when the sun shines, Psalm 84:2; John 3:14-20.

   4. The light directs our way, and we are influenced by the objects which we view, to avoid what appears odious or dangerous, and to pursue what we think is agreeable with all our might. So by faith the soul flies to Christ to supply all its wants, and cleaves to Him in the way of holiness, and is moved to watch against all iniquity, and to crucify the flesh, with its affections and lusts: This was the whole tenor of my book, which therefore I entitled, *True Faith Will Produce*

Good Works; but this title Mr. *Martin* denies, and attempts to prove the contrary; though before he proceeds to any proof, he again brings up his frightful imagination, if possible to prepossess the reader's mind. But hoping that the reader will not be guilty of the folly of judging a matter before he hears it, I would desire him to take notice what it is that is now to be proved. It is, that "*True faith* does sometimes fail of producing good works," p. 25. *True faith*, which I describe to be "A receiving with *all the heart* the witness and testimony that God has given us." Faith by which the soul views "The *precept* to be true and excellent, therefore to be obeyed; the *promise* to be sure and sufficient, therefore he shall be supported, and presents eternal things as *near* and *real*, therefore to be regarded without delay," p. 33, 35, of my book. This is the constant idea that I gave of true faith; yet the first text that my opponent brings to prove that it sometimes fails of producing good works, is John 12:42-43, which inform us of some rulers who believed on Jesus, but did not confess Him, because they loved the praise of men more than the praise of God. His second is John 8:30-32, where we find some Jews who had a sort of belief on *Jesus*, but He signified to them that a *continuance* in His word would discover whether they were His *disciples indeed* or not; and that discovery was soon made, for His only telling of them that they should *know the truth*, and the *truth should make them free*, raised their resentment. Now if men can believe the gospel with *all their hearts*, and yet love the praise of men more than the praise of God, if they can be *true believers*, and yet not *know the truth*, nor be *made free* by it, then he has proved his point; if not, he has done nothing towards it.

To introduce his next proof he tells us, that love is a labor, and we may be sure that it is a work which God will not forget, Heb. 6:10, and then turns us to 1st Cor. 13:2, in order to prove that true faith may be without love, p. 26. But it is pity the man had not read on to the next verse, which contains as much of a proof that giving *all our goods to feed the poor* may be without *love*, as the other does that a faith of miracles may be without it; and both prove that all external works or gifts will not avail us, without they are done from right principles; but how does that prove that true faith will not produce love and good works? In the last verse of that chapter the Apostle sets faith before charity, and in *Gal.* 5:6, he says, *Faith works by love,* and I wonder how Mr. *Martin* thinks any can love and serve God here but only by faith, since those objects are invisible to sense. *Peter* shows, that the way in which saints *love* and *rejoice* in an *unseen* Christ, is by *believing,* 1st *Pet.* 1:8, and *Paul* shows *faith unfeigned, as* well as charity, to be so essential to true obedience, that all teaching that *swerves* there-from he calls *vain jangling, 1st Tim.* 1:5-7, and I leave others to judge, who are now guilty of such ignorant jangling.

To finish his proofs, our author turns us to the many nominal believers in our land, whose faith does not produce good works; to which he might have seen an answer in my 57th page, where I observed that the Apostle *James* compares such a faith to a *dead body;* but who would reject all bodies, because there are some dead stinking ones? We read of the *spirit of faith,* and of *living by faith*; and those pretenders to faith and grace who do not live so, *Jude* calls them *filthy dreamers;* but who will argue that our waking views do not govern our conduct, because *dreams* do not commonly bring men off from their sluggish beds! *Paul* says to some bad professors among the Christians, *"Awake to righteousness and sin not; for some have not the knowledge of God: I speak this to your shame!"* It is a shame to any church to suffer such members among them (1st Cor. 15:34). Again, to the saints at *Rome* he says, *"It is high time ye awake out of sleep"* and whenever they are awaked to the exercise of true faith, it will as certainly produce good works in every soul, as it moved *Abraham* to give up his darling at the divine command, or *Moses* to count reproaches for Christ, greater riches than all the treasures in *Egypt*, and enabled him to endure, as seeing Him that is invisible.

Before Mr. *Martin* began his remarks upon my piece, he entered a caution against being deceived by the power of tradition, p. 4, but he is not the first man who has been ensnared in the very thing he cautioned others against.

Tradition has taught him to hold the six principles in Heb. 6:1, [Editor's note: This remark identifies Mr. Martin as a "Six-Principle Baptist", and if pastor of Rehoboth Church in the Philadelphia Association, he was a Welsh Baptist.] as a summary of Christian doctrine and practice, instead of viewing them as so many articles of the *Jewish* creed; and this has not a little influence in leading him into mistakes about faith; for though he allows that faith sometimes comprehends the whole counsel of God, yet he says, "Faith sometimes comprehends only one of the principles of the doctrine of Christ, as in Heb. 6:1." And after saying much upon it, he declares, that "God has not promised eternal life upon that single grace of faith, as it is the belief of the truth, and one of the principles of the doctrine of Christ", p. 18, 19, as if faith was but the sixth part of religion; which is so far from truth, that the sacred writer goes on, in the eleventh chapter of this same epistle, to show that all the good which was ever done by ancient saints, was done *by faith.* One of those principles, viz., *laying on of hands*, has caused a great deal of controversy, both formerly and latterly; and we are informed by one who was no enemy to the practice, that it came among the Baptists from the "Established church, who use it under the name of *confirmation* (NOTE: Mr. *Crosby's* History of the *English Baptist,* vol. IV, page 291.)." I do not mention this, as though I thought their holding it as a tradition, or the *Romanists* holding it as one of the *Seven Sacraments*, was a sufficient evidence against the practice, but only to put each one upon examination, whether they stand upon any thing better than tradition or not; neither shall I meddle here with that controversy, farther than it concerns this text, for many things may be contained elsewhere, which are not in such a particular text; though since such great mistakes concerning faith and salvation are drawn from this, I think it is a loud call to examine, whether we have not mistaken its true meaning. The general rule given us to go by is to compare spiritual things with spiritual. Now an evident design of the epistle to the *Hebrews,* was to explain to them the types of the ceremonial law, and show their *perfect* fulfillment in Jesus Christ; but the sacred writer complains in the fifth chapter, that they were dull of hearing, and were like *babes* that had need of one to teach them *again*, which were the *first principles* of the oracles of God; and having observed that those who are of full age, have their senses exercised to discern both good and evil, he begins the sixth chapter with calling them to *leave* the principles of the doctrine of Christ, and go on to *perfection.* Dr. Gill on the place says, the word translated *first principles*, is the same word that in Gal. 4:3, 9, is rendered *elements*, by which it is very evident that the ceremonies of the law are intended; and both there and here, Christians are reproved for their *childish* fondness for them.

Letters are the elements, or first principles of learning, which *we* teach children; but we expect them afterwards to *leave* their spelling, and go on to a more *perfect* manner of reading: So the first principles of the doctrine of Christ were taught by the *letters* of that law, which are all now clearly to be read in Him who is the glorious WORD. Under the law they were to spell out the doctrine of *repentance from dead works,* by slain beasts, and confessing their sins over them; of *faith towards God,* as the God of *Israel,* in covenant with them; of cleansing from pollution, by the divers *baptisms* or *bathings,* which were commanded; of the laying our sins upon Jesus, by the *laying on of hands* on the sacrifice, which was enjoined not less than a dozen times in *Leviticus;* the *resurrection from the dead* was shadowed out by the two goats for a sin-offering, one of which was to die, and the other be let go alive; some intimations also were then given of *eternal judgment,* but since the New Testament has taught us *repentance,* by looking on Him whom we have pierced, to *believe* on the Lord Jesus Christ for salvation, who saves by the *washing* of regeneration, and renewing of the Holy Ghost: has taught us that our sins were *laid* on Christ, who bore them in His own body on the tree, died for our offenses, and *rose again* for our justification, and will come again to *judge* the world in righteousness. Since these things are clearly opened in the gospel, shall we still be fond of the elements of the law? No, let us *leave* them, and go on to *perfection;* with which compare Chapter 8:9-12, which show that the service of the tabernacle was *a figure* for the time then present, in which were offered both gifts and sacrifices, that could not make him that did the service *perfect,* as pertaining to the conscience, which stood only in meats and drinks, and divers *washings,* and carnal ordinances, imposed on them until the time of reformation; but Christ being come an high priest of good things to come, by a greater and more perfect tabernacle, etc., the words *perfect* and *perfection* appear constantly to be used in this epistle, to distinguish the *substantial* blessings of the gospel from the *shadows* of the law, as in Chapter 7:11, 19 and 10:1, 14. I find also, that the word in Chapter 9:10, which is rendered *washings,* is *baptisms* (NOTE: See Dr. *Gill,* and other expositors on the place. Mr. *Purver,* in his late translation of the Bible, translates the word *baptisms* here as he does in the sixth chapter.), in the plural number, as it is here in the sixth chapter; but the singular, *baptism,* is used about twenty times for an ordinance of the gospel, and never once in the plural, as I can find, in all the New Testament; which is a further evidence, that these six principles are not a summary of the gospel, but of the ceremonies of the law: And if it is not so, how can we account for it, that repentance and faith should be named, and not hope and love? Or, that baptism should be expressed, and not a word of the Lord's Supper, which is equally an ordinance of the gospel?

If then repentance and faith are held in the language of *Moses,* rather than *Paul,* no wonder if the veil remains upon such hearts, so that they cannot with open face behold the glories of divine grace in Jesus Christ; and is not this the cause *of* our Mr. Martin saying, "Shall we live by faith without works, or shall we build our hope upon faith and obedience, and not on faith only?" p. 20. Answer, he that builds his hope either upon faith or obedience, or upon both together, considered as our acts, builds upon the sand; for *"other foundation can no man lay than that is laid, which is Christ Jesus;"* and if we are enabled to build upon Him, still the whole weight of all that is built must rest upon that Eternal Rock. Mr. *Martin* proceeds to cite a large number of Scriptures, which prove that all men will finally partake of the fruit of their doings, and then says, "I have been the more particular upon this great duty of good works, because there are many in these latter days, that seem to have little or no dependence upon good works in order to salvation. It is true, they will allow that good works are necessary to adorn a disciple, but not to make a disciple of Christ, though our Lord saith, so shall ye be my disciples, that is in bearing much fruit," p. 23. This is too plain to require much answer, though if the old gentleman should live till next fall, I should be glad if he would go into a good orchard, and examine carefully among all the trees, *adorned* with good fruit, whether he can find any fruit that *made* the tree good which it grows upon, or whether the tree does not evidence by this fruit, that it was a good tree before? And also to consider well, whether the way to promote its future fruitfulness would be to turn up its *roots,* that it might now stand upon its lovely fruit! If he will then be pleased to read the following texts, I suppose he will have a sufficient answer: Matt. 12:33; Rom. 11:18.

However, since he holds that good works *make* disciples, and represents that we hold other wise, because we would obtain eternal life in a way "Easier than to cut off the right hand; or pluck out the right eye, or to deny self and take up our cross, and follow Christ in the strait and narrow way," p. 21. I shall bring things a little nearer home; for if I am not much mistaken, this very man holds the external acts of baptism, and laying on of hands, which are done but *once* in a person's life, to be so essential to *make* disciples, that he will have no sort of religious fellowship with any without them, while those who have them are freely received to his communion, though they have no visible worship *daily* in their families, nor *weekly* regard to the Lord's day, only in time of worship; not withstanding the same sacred writer who calls us to *leave Jewish* principles concerning Christ, tells us that there *remaineth a rest* (or *Sabbath*, as the margin has it) to the people of God, Chapter 4:9. Now observe:

1. his naming the *seventh day,* and then speaking of *another day*, which *remaineth*, and giving a like reason to enforce the latter, as was given to enforce the former, plainly implies that a particular day of the week is referred to in both; for in verse 4 he recites the reason by which the seventh day was enforced, and then to enforce this rest that remaineth, says in verse 10, "*For HE that is entered into his*

rest, HE also hath ceased from his own works, AS GOD did from His." And as it is certain that the Son rested from the work of redemption on the *first day*, as the Father did from the work of creation on the *seventh*, who will dare to say that He, *He also,* that *rested* as GOD *did*, can mean any other than the Son, whom all men are required to *honour, even AS they honour the Father?* John 5:23.

2. It is readily granted, that the Apostle's aim is to engage souls to *hear* and *believe* the gospel, whereby they *enter into* spiritual *rest* here, and eternal *rest* hereafter, which as much exceeds the rest which *Jesus,* i.e., *Joshua,* gave *Israel* in *Canaan,* as heaven exceeds earth; the *gospel* which *first gives rest* to *heavy laden souls*, in order that they might take Christ's *yoke,* and *work* for him, Matt. 11:28, while the *law* enjoined *six days work* before their *rest* on the *seventh,* and the long *fatigues* of the wilderness, before their *rest* in *Canaan*: But how can the gospel be heard without a *preacher*, Rom. 10-14, and without a *time* to meet for that purpose? Hence after our apostle had shown, that the worship instituted by Christ was as much superior to that appointed by *Moses,* as the Son is superior to a servant, and that Christ's house is his church, he immediately began his comment upon *David's* words, which reach down to the place we are now upon; the tenor of all which is, to show the importance of hearing and regarding the *voice* of Christ in His gospel, and which is preached in His church, in this language, *"Today, if ye will hear his voice, harden not*

your hearts." And though this should be the preacher's language in season and out of season, 2nd Tim. 4:2, yet that is so far from disproving the appointment of a *stated season* for worship under the gospel, that it strongly implies such an appointment. For as our apostle began this subject, with observing the superiority of the worship appointed in the Christian church, to that of the *Jews; so* he calls us in verse 14 to *hold fast our profession;* not only our faith, but also our profession of it; which call is renewed in Chapter 10:23-25, with a further explanation of how it is to be done, namely, by *considering one another, to provoke unto love and good works; not forsaking the assembling of ourselves together, as the manner of some is; but exhorting one another,* etc. Neither meetings, days, nor ordinances, can be observed aright without faith; and if we are true believers, we *are come to the General Assembly, and church of the first born, which are written in heaven,* Chapter 12:22-23. And in the same chapter we are commanded to make *strait paths for our feet;* but what *crooked* work do men make, if they take internals to exclude externals, or externals to exclude internals, or put one for the other, to suit their own turn? And may we not as justly say, because we *are come* by faith to the *general assembly of the church,* that therefore we have no warrant for external church assemblies, as to argue, because we which have believed *do enter into rest,* that therefore no particular day now *remaineth* for Christians to *rest* in from all worldly affairs, notwithstanding the text expressly speaks of *another day* which *remaineth* to the people of God, distinct from the *seventh,* enforced with a like reason as that was?

Again, though some make much use of *Paul's* caution against letting any man judge us in respect of an *holy-day, new-moon, sabbath-days, or ordinances;* yet how plain is it, that he is there speaking of the *hand-writing of ordinances,* which Christ took *out of the way, nailing it to his cross,* and so could not be retained in Christian worship, only by the *traditions* and *commandments* of *men? Col. 2:14-22.* But how *crooked* is it, to take what was spoken against *Jewish* ceremonies, to exclude gospel ordinances, or the observation of the Lord's day? In the same chapter the apostle says, *"Though I be absent in the flesh, yet am I with you in the spirit, joying and beholding your order";* and another apostle says, *"Ye need not that any man teach you, but as the same anointing teacheth you of all things";* what warrant then have men or women to meet externally, to teach others, or hear others teach them? Let this be fairly answered, and we do not fear having as good an answer in the case before us.

Jewish ordinances were types of things to come, but Christian ordinances are memorials of what is already done, and to stir us up to a right behavior towards God, and towards each other; therefore let us never take what was written against the ceremonies of the law, to exclude any appointment of the gospel: And since the Son of God rested from the work of purchasing our redemption, on the first day of the week, and we have the example of his disciples meeting on that day, for worship, and to break bread, John 20:19, 26; Acts 20:7. Since the saint's liberality, which is an *odour of a sweet smell, a sacrifice acceptable, well-pleasing to God,* was commanded to be offered on that day, Phil. 4:18; 1st Cor. 16:2, and as a table and supper, set apart from a common to a sacred use, is called the *Lord's table,* and the *Lord's Supper,* so we have a day called the *Lord's day, Rev. 1:10;* therefore let us all *regard the day* to him.

Again our apostle says, "*We have an altar* (by which he evidently means Christ) *by Him therefore let us offer the sacrifice of praise to God* CONTINUALLY, *that is, the fruit of our lips, giving thanks to His name",* Heb. 13:10, 15, and as this was written to the *Hebrews,* who can doubt of his having reference here to their *morning* and *evening sacrifice,* which they were commanded to offer upon the altar, *day by day continually---a continual* burnt offering throughout their generations, Exod. 29:38, 42, which is afterward called the *continual* burnt offering, not less than ten times in two chapters, (NOTE: Levit. 28 & 29, See more of this in my sermon on Family Prayer.)? And take notice, this spiritual sacrifice is required to be offered *continually* with our *lips*; and what can that mean less than vocal addresses to the throne of grace, as often as their morning and evening offerings were? especially when we remember that our Lord has taught his disciples to pray after this manner, *Our Father*, ---give us *this day* our daily bread; not this week, this month, or this year, but *this day*; how plainly does it imply our duty to come, not only personally in secret, but also unitedly in our families, to *our* Father, *every day*? We are also commanded to *pray always with all prayer*, Eph. 6:18, and surely, *all prayer* includes family prayer as well as other.

Having given a little sketch of the scripture authority for these duties, I can freely leave it with every conscience to judge, whether it looks more like *denying self*, and taking up our *cross daily*, to rise from our beds in the morning, and return to them again at night; to go to, and return from, our food, with no more visible acknowledgment of our great Preserver and Benefactor than the ox that eateth grass; than it does to realize how dependent we are upon Him continually, so as to have our prayer *daily* come up before Him as incense, and the lifting up of our hands as the evening sacrifice, and whenever we *eat,* to *give God thanks,* Rom. 14:6. And whether it looks more like plucking out a right eye, or cutting off a right hand, to make God's house so much a house of *merchandise,* as to carry *our worldly schemes* even into the intermission of worship on the *Lord's day,* and not wait till the day is over, before we begin to *sell corn,* and *set forth wheat,* than it does to *regard the whole day* as *holy to the Lord, and honorable,* and *honor Him, not doing our own ways, nor finding our own pleasure, nor speaking our own words.* And though many are hypocritical while they pretend to these duties, yet may it not well appear surprising, to see any professed Christians make that an excuse for their own neglect, which is the same excuse that infidels make for their neglect of all religion! as if other's wrongs would excuse us from doing right!

How far tradition may have ensnared and blinded good men, with respect to these things, I do not pretend to say: I have experienced enough in other traditions, to teach me the importance of treating all men with candor and charity, and yet to abhor the *lukewarmness* which many would cover under those lovely names, whereby religion is treated as if it was only a piece of state policy, that might be turned into any shape, as occasion or interest suited. Charity is love to God and man, which moves the soul to reverence our Creator, and to regard our fellow-creatures in their several stations and relations; and all dispositions and actions contrary thereto are sin, let men call them what they will. *Charity rejoiceth not in iniquity, but rejoiceth in the truth,* and therefore moves those who are under its influence to exert themselves in their several stations, to promote the cause of truth in the world. And since the custom of casting off fear, and restraining prayer before God, greatly prevails in our nation and land, and also of profaning the Lord's day with carnal schemes, ease or diversions; and many strengthen themselves therein, by the loose principles and conduct of some teachers and professors, surely it is high time for us all to awake, and bear a more bold testimony against such ways than has yet been done. What! shall we, under a pretense of owning every day to be the Lord's, rob Him of a great part, or the whole, of the one day that is consecrated for His worship! What! under a pretense of *spiritual* worship, shall we indulge our *carnal* ease and inclinations, till some awakening Providence, or powerful influence, pulls us from our sluggish beds! Shall a pretense of *heart-worship* any more be brought to excuse the neglect of *confessing with our mouths,* and *daily* offering to God the fruit of our *lips,* giving thanks to His name! The apostle *James's* language to the pretenders to faith and invisible religion in his day was, *"Shew me thy faith without thy works, and I will shew thee my faith by my works."* So now, show to thy family, if thou canst, that thou dost believe all good things come from God, while they rarely, *if* ever, hear thee worship Him, or give Him thanks there-for! Show to any man, if you can, that you believe every day to be the Lord's, while you don't keep one day to Him, without filling a great part of it with *your own ways,* and *your own pleasures!*

The great point which brought ruin upon the *Jews,* was their refusing to *render to God the fruits of His vineyard in their seasons*; but instead of it, abusing His servants, and then killing His Son, with this aim, ---*The inheritance shall be ours,* Matt. 21:33-41; Mark 12:1-9. And alas! how much of the same disposition is working at this day, to try to get time, and all its advantages, to be *ours*! Surely their *desolate* land, which *enjoys her sabbaths*, Levit. 26:34, 43, calls like thunder to us, to beware of such ways, left, as we have greater light, we bring on ourselves, and our land, a greater vengeance than they did. Indeed 'tis common for persons now to exclaim against the old *Pharisees*, for their hypocrisy, *selfishness* and cruelty (just as they did against others, Matt. 23:29-31) while they discover sad tokens of their going in the same way, by seeking life, *not by faith, but as it were by the deeds of the law*; which deeds yet are only some *lesser matters*, while *justice, mercy* and *faithfulness*, are neglected.

How far our author, or any of his admirers are guilty in any of these respects, I don't pretend to determine, but leave that to God and their own consciences; and am far from thinking myself better by nature than they: Yet who can hear men tell of, "building their hope upon their faith and obedience"; of "Dependence upon good works in order to salvation", and that our good works not only adorn, but also "Make disciples of Christ", and not warn them of their danger! This is so far from the good old way to heaven, that Job, who was a perfect and upright walker, yet upon a near view of the divine Being, cried out, *"Behold I am vile!"* and again, *"I abhor myself!"* So far was he from trusting to himself or his doings, Job 1:1; 40:4; and 43:6. The man after God's own heart was so far from building his hope upon his faith, or his works, that he says, *"I will go in the strength of the Lord God; I will make mention of thy righteousness, even of thine ONLY"*, Psalm 71:5, 16. A near view of a holy God, caused that eminent saint, the prophet Isaiah, to cry out, *"Wo is me, for I am undone, because I am a man of unclean lips!"* and nothing could relieve him but a living application from God's altar, by which his iniquity was taken away, and his sin purged; which moved him to ready obedience, saying, *"Here am I, send me"*. He would not go of his own head, but was ready to obey the divine call, Isaiah 6:5-8. So now, we must all have our conscience purged from dead works, by Christ's blood, in order to serve the living God, Heb. 9:14. The character of gospel believers is, they worship God in the spirit, rejoice in Christ Jesus, and have NO confidence in the flesh; that is, in their own doings: And they are warned to beware of all that teach otherwise, as creatures that are both odious and dangerous, Phil. 3:2-3.

PART---II

Wherein is opened the Consistency *and* Duty *of holding forth Divine Sovereignty, and Man's Impotency, while yet we address their Consciences with the Warnings of Truth, and Calls of the Gospel.*

AFTER I had written the principal part of that discourse upon faith, which I have now been vindicating, Mr. *Sandeman's* letters were put into my hands, with a request that I would carefully examine them, and remark on what I discovered to be amiss; in doing of which, some things appeared to me to be of so dangerous a nature, that I thought it a duty to expose them publicly; and accordingly inserted a few remarks in my introduction, referring to the body of the discourse for a positive opening of my views of the right way. But a number of people, not observing that in a note, page 25, I had thus referred them forward, and supposing that the grand design of my writing was against him, have accused me of the same crime I charged upon him, viz. of only picking out what was wrong in writers, and passing over what was right. Whereas my first and main design had no concern with him, and as he owns that he has adopted the good sentiments of others, "Without quoting them, or mentioning their names," how could I do justice in reciting them as his, when I knew not whose they were ? Therefore I cited one excellent passage, and then endeavored to point out some of the most dangerous snares that I discovered in his writings, referring to the following discourse to explain my views of the truth. Nevertheless I freely acknowledge, that my love of brevity left some things in too much obscurity, especially upon the distinction between doctrinal and experimental knowledge. My idea of the difference is, that a person may truly be slain by the law, and made alive by the gospel, and yet not know, perhaps not have a thought, that what he has experienced is the change called *conversion*; but doctrinal teaching may be a means of opening clearly to him, that it is the very change described in scripture by that name. Christ's disciples had experienced *the way* of access to the Father, yet they denied that they *knew* it, when he mentioned it under that name, John 14:4-5. On the other hand, men may learn to talk orthodoxly or critically concerning these things, while they do not truly know them. This is the distinction I meant, and the occasion of mentioning it was, his representing that a man could not have "Known and preached, trusted, and loved the Lord Jesus Christ for many years", if now his mind was relieved and his views more cleared by his writings; and I still think that representation to be false: But I used one expression that I now utterly retract, viz, right notions in the head, without knowing the truth in the heart;

for I believe right ideas will always produce right effects upon our hearts and lives, and that all men's notions about truth, which do not produce such effects, are not *right* notions; but a holding the *truth in unrighteousness,* and *changing truth into a lie;* and those who receive not the love of the truth will be damned, because they *believe not the truth;* but *believe a lie, Rom. 1:18, 25; 2nd Thess. 2:10-12,* and one well observes that perhaps the lie they believed was, "That if they did penance, and performed a number of good duties, they should by that means procure an interest in the justifying righteousness of Christ." And how much has this strong delusion spread through the world! Indeed the modes of *doing* are very different, some placing it more in *external* forms, others in *internal* exercises; and though they seem to differ greatly, yet how many agree in *doing for life,* instead of *receiving all by faith,* that they may *live unto God!* Probably some will say, these are Mr *Sandeman's* sentiments: I know he suggests many such things in his writings, and I would never oppose truth there any more than elsewhere; but I have seen as good wheat laid to bait a net, as that which is laid up in the garner; and an apprehension of a snare for souls, baited with choice truths and keen turns of wit, was the only occasions of my writing against him; which snare appears in such terms as these, "Assurance of hope is enjoyed only ' by those who give all diligence to obtain it, in the self-denied works of obedience"; and he says, "No man can be charged with the sin of disbelieving the gospel, for *doubting* if he be a good Christian; his chief hazard lies on the other side"; yet in answer to his friend's request of a clearer explanation of this point, he says, "We must not consider the person advancing to the assurance of hope, as engaged in a certain round of duties, so as his comfort should arise from a *consciousness* of his performing, or designing to perform, them from *right motives,* let them be called motives arising from the faith, or by any other name: Thus the Christian profession would become a *Pharisaical* scheme (NOTE: Epistolary Correspondence, *Glasgow* edition, page 86.)." This is so far from truth, that if we could speak with the tongues of men and angels, if we could understand all mysteries and all knowledge, and perform the *self-denied works* of giving all our goods to feed the poor, and our bodies to the flames, yet unless these were performed from a *good principle,* and *right motives,* we should still *be nothing*, and all our doings *profit us nothing"* (1st Cor. 13:1-3). And though he asserts, that "A person by being brought to the knowledge of the truth, is not thereby led to think himself possessed of some *good principles*, by which he stands more nearly *related to God* than he was, or than other men; his comfort does not lie in thinking on any thing about himself, or any *change* he has undergone; but he is comforted in thinking on what is *without* him, on what is *absent* from him, even on what is in heaven (NOTE: *Ibid.* page 82, 83.)." Yet *Paul* shows that the *good principle of charity* out of a *pure heart, good conscience*, and *faith unfeigned,* is so essential to obedience, that he who *swerves* there-from, understands neither *what he says nor whereof he affirms*; and that the saint is comforted in his near *relation to God,* by having the *spirit of adoption sent into his heart;* and also by beholding the divine glories, whereby he is *changed into the same image;* and he calls professors to *examine* themselves, for they ought to *know* that Christ is IN *them,* except they are *reprobates,* 1st *Tim.* 1:5-7; Rom. 8:15; 2nd Cor. 3:18 and 13:5. 5. This is so far from a *Pharisaical scheme,* that the very nature of the *Pharisees* scheme was, to make a great pretence of self-denial and *outward* obedience, without any regard to an *inward change,* or acting from *right motives.*

And though the plan now before us talks much of the cross and self-denial, yet it is so much more self-pleasing than the *carnal ordinances* of the law, that the law appointed but *three feasts* in a year for all the church to meet at; but this plan appoints *fifty-two,* and "Cannot allow any member to be absent from the *feast,* either through indifference, or mere inconvenience": And tacitly brands all with the name of *Pharisees,* who are against encouraging *all diversions* public or private, which are not connected with circumstances *really sinful:* Which by the way, would brand Solomon with that odious epithet, who after a thorough experience of such *diversions* says, "It is *better* to go to the house of *mourning* than to the house of *feasting;* for the heart of the *wise* is in the house of mourning; but the heart of *fools* is in the house of *mirth*": And it would condemn *Paul,* who was in *fasting often,* and says, Let your *moderation* be known to *all men*; and let us, who are of *the day, be sober,* Eccl. 7:2-4; 2nd Cor. 11:27; Phil. 4:5; 1st Thes. 5:8. Again Mr. *Sandeman* represents, that our writers in general upon the steps of the Spirit's work in conviction and conversion, are much more hurtful to mankind, than writers of *romances;* and that the *pulpit* at present does *more hurt* than the *stage;* and spends eighteen pages artfully to represent, that the "Deity makes little account of our thoughts through all the busy scenes of life"; but will likely receive condemned felons, at the end of it, into his kingdom (NOTE: Letters on *Theron,* etc., vol. II, page 40, etc., also page 61, 103.)." These are the dangerous snares laid for souls, that occasioned my writing against him, and not from any delight in controversy with him or others; nor from any apprehension that his form of a church could greatly prevail, which casts out every member that does not concur with the church in every circumstance; for as an excellent author observes, "It is hardly conceivable, that a great number of men should *exactly* agree upon a great number of different points, without *any* variation, unless they *contrive* to agree together for the sake of carrying on some particular scheme (NOTE: Thoughts on Education, by the author of *Britain's Remembrancer*, page 16.)."

How far his scheme has had an influence on many to neglect all church-fellowship, because they cannot find a perfect church in this wilderness; and how far it has emboldened sinners to treat all awakening preaching and writings with scorn and neglect, rather following stage-plays, romances, or other devices of their own hearts, with hopes still of being received into the kingdom of heaven at last; and if conscience galls them, to try to ease it with some critical speculations, or outward forms, stifling convictions of their hypocrisy, with the conceit that *doubting* is a good sign, and that to be concerned to know whether we have experienced a saving *change;* so as to act from *good principles,* is *Pharisaical!* I say, how far his scheme has influenced these things, I leave with the Judge before whom we must all soon appear; but as legalists and libertines both charge those with inconsistency, who hold forth the doctrine of man's impotency and divine sovereignty, and yet earnestly address their consciences with the warnings of truth, and calls of the gospel, and as false *imaginations* concerning this matter are the strongest *hold* that Satan has left, to keep his *goods in peace*, I shall a little further offer my mite towards pulling it down: In order to which, it is needful to take brief survey of the nature both of the law and gospel.

As to the law , our Lord has given us a summary of it, in as clear terms as can be used: *"Thou shalt love the Lord thy God with all thy heart, soul, and all thy mind, and thy neighbor as thyself.---This do and thou shalt live," Luke 10:27-28.* Love is the temper of happiness, and without it there can be none, and the nobler its object the greater the happiness, and the easier to obey the precept; how holy, just, and good, then is this law, which requires our highest love to the supreme fountain of being and excellency, and our subordinate love to all other beings, according to their relation and connection to Him and to us? This law then constituted a union of heart between the whole system of rational beings, which influenced to all right behavior toward each other, according to their several stations and relations; and the fruit of such behavior is, *"This do and thou shalt live."* Hence learn,

I. That the nature of this law is immutable and perpetual, and it is as vain for any one soul to think of ever being exempted for one moment from obligation to love God with all the heart, and our neighbor as ourselves, as to think of dethroning Him, or annihilating our own souls; for as long as we remain His creatures, 'tis impossible but that we must remain under obligation to love and obey him.

2. Here we may learn the true nature of sin; it is the *transgression of this law;* it is a revolt from the Creator, and setting up the creature in his stead, *Rom.* 1:25. Hence we are told, that of the three *Hebrew* words ordinarily used for it, transgression signifies *rebellion*; iniquity, *crookedness, perverseness;* and sin, a *missing the mark* (NOTE: Dr. *Gill's* Exposition of Psalm 51:1-2.). And surely the source of all our woes was a *rebellion* against our rightful King and Lawgiver, and turning aside to our

own *crooked, perverse* ways, whereby we *miss the mark* both of our duty and happiness; and the immediate consequence was loss of union and communion with God, which is *spiritual death*; innumerable evils in this world, that at length dissolve the union between soul and body, which is *natural death;* and finally will be the casting of soul and body into the burning lake, which is *eternal death*; all which are the just *wages of sin.* And mark it, death is to be always viewed according to its nature; the death of a rational soul is as different from that of the body, as spirit is from clay; the body without union with the soul can do nothing at all; the soul without union with God can do nothing right; but a soul *dead in sin* still *walks,* and is sometimes more active than a saint, and for this plain reason, the sinner's powers are all bent one way, while the saint has in him, as it were, the company of two armies, so that the children of this world are in their generation *wiser than the children of light, Luke* 16:8; *Eph.* 2:1-2. Hence all attempts to represent addresses to sinners consciences, to be like addresses to senseless carcasses, are attempts *to darken counsel*, and belong to the kingdom of darkness.

3. How vain are men's hopes of getting life by their own *doings,* in any shape whatever? Christ says, *THIS DO and thou shalt live*; it is not "*wouldings,*"(sic) promises or endeavours, that will avail without *doing*, doing *this*; *this* perfect, *this* universal, *this* immutable law of love; *love* to God and man, *love* with all our *soul* and *mind*, as well as

strength. Therefore the law is *spiritual*, but we are *carnal*; all inclinations as well as actions that are contrary, or that do not come up to this law of love, are sin; hence our Lord, upon occasion of a lovely youth who had shown an outward regard to the law all his days, and yet had such a love to this world, that he would not part with it for Christ, declared to his disciples, that it is *easier for a camel to go through the eye of a needle*, than for such a man to enter into the kingdom of heaven; but they being astonished, he adds, *with man it is impossible, but not with God*, Mark 10:17-27. Two things make it *impossible* with man, one is, he cannot make up his past breach of the law, and the other is, he cannot now turn his heart from earth to heaven, though God can do both; which brings us,

4. To the nature and design of the gospel. Man was become a *rebel* against the eternal King, by breaking the best of all laws, by which he had forfeited life, and was neither able to satisfy for his crime, nor to change his own heart; therefore the King's Son engaged to do the one, and the Holy Spirit to effect the other; not by abating the law, as some vainly dream; no, Jesus warns us against such a *thought,* and declares, that *Till heaven and earth pass, one JOT or one TITTLE shall in no wise pass from the law, till ALL be fulfilled, Matt.* 5:18. He fulfilled it by taking the rebels place, and obeying and suffering for our sins, *"The just for the unjust, that He might bring us unto God, that we might be made the righteousness of God in him;"* that God

might be *"just, and the justifier of him which believeth in Jesus"*; might justify the *ungodly*, Rom. 3:26 and 4:5; 2nd Cor. 5:18-20; 1st Peter 3:18. In consequence of which, the gospel *proclaims liberty to prisoners* and *captives*, Isaiah 61:1; Luke 6:18. Surely not an exemption from the King's authority and government! No; but liberty from the just sentence of *death*, from Satan's *tyranny*, and from the *bondage of corruption*, into the glorious *liberty of the sons of God*; liberty to serve him in *newness of spirit,* and *not in the oldness of the letter*, Rom. 7:6. The oldness of the letter was, *"The man that doth them shall live in them;" " this do and thou shalt live;" "but cursed is every one that continueth not" to do all.* The newness of the spirit is, Christ delivers from the *curse*, and gives the covenant blessings of the Spirit, and writes the laws in our *hearts,* with this tenor *I will,* and *they shall,* Gal. 3:10-14; *Heb.* 8:10. The oldness of the letter promised life upon doing, but gave no strength to do; the newness of the Spirit says, "As thy days, so shall thy strength be;" my grace is sufficient for thee; I will never leave thee, nor forsake thee: It calls us to come boldly to the throne of grace for all the help we need. The oldness of the letter gives no encouragement to come only upon our own doings, and sets a flaming sword in the way of the guilty; but the newness of the spirit directs us to take all our encouragement to come, from the merits, intercession and promise of our great High Priest, who has engaged *justice* and *faithfulness* to *forgive* the guilty, and to *cleanse* the filthy, Heb. 4:14-16; 1st John 1:9. As the strength of sin is the law, the letter arms the *accuser* against the soul that daily breaks it; but the Spirit enables the believer to *overcome* him, by the *blood* of the Lamb, and by such a view of heavenly glories, as to carry their *love* even above *life* itself, Rev. 12:11. In a word, the *letter killeth*, but the *Spirit giveth life*, 2nd Cor. 3:6.

Yet notwithstanding this distinction is written so plain that he may run that reads it, many still dwell upon the oldness of the letter, and reckon it "Strange and unaccountable, that any should assert that there is nothing to be *done by sinners in order* to their salvation, beside believing (NOTE: Dr. *Mayhew's* sermons on striving to enter the strait gate, page 31, 32.)!" as if they had never read Rom. 3:28 and 4:5.

I suppose this author has stated this point as fairly as any have done on that side of the question. He says, "The question is, whether unregenerated sinners, under the dispensation of the gospel, have *any* day of grace and salvation afforded to them, in such a sense, that they shall certainly obtain eternal life, provided they heartily desire it, and strive to that end?" And he asserts, that "There is a certain connection between sinners striving to obtain the salvation which God has revealed, and their actually obtaining it (NOTE: *Ibid.* page 46.).

But what is the salvation that God has revealed? It is from *enemies* to be *reconciled* and *saved* by his Son, Rom.

5:10. And what is there to be *done* by sinners, in *order* to *this* salvation? Their rebellion is atoned for by the King's Son, and He *beseeches* and *prays* them to be *reconciled*; how then can the sinner *heartily desire this* salvation, and yet have something to *do*, before he obtains it? 2nd Cor. 5:20. And what do men mean by a "day of grace," if 'tis the day in which the King proclaims the gospel way of reconciliation, and sends His servants to preach to sinners, and His spirit *strive* with them, while His long-suffering *waits*; yet ever with this language, "Behold, NOW is the accepted time, behold, NOW is *the day* of salvation! Come, for all things are *now ready*," 1st Pet. 3:18-20; 2nd Cor. 6:2; Luke 14:17. Such a day of grace we readily grant all sinners under the light of the gospel have. But if the gospel says, *Come, all things are now ready*, and the Spirit *strives* to convince the sinner of the truth of it; I desire to know what the sinner's *striving* is before he comes? We all know, that *striving* implies *resistance* of one against another; and those who in ancient time enquired so often what they *should do, Stephen* plainly told them to their heads what they *did do* : " —Ye *do always resist the Holy Ghost, Acts* 7:51.

There can be no half-way; the instant we believe the gospel, we are reconciled to God, and unite in striving against all His and our enemies, *striving* according to His working in and by us, Col. 1:29; Phil. 3:14. And if we are not united with him, we *believe* not the *truth*, but have *pleasure* in *unrighteousness*, let us talk of speculative faith, or good desires, what we will, 2nd Thes. 2:12. And to talk of repentance before faith, is more absurd still; for who ever was sorry for any action, before he believed it to be some way disagreeable! It is conviction of the *truth* of the law that causes legal repentance, and looking by *faith* on Him whom we have pierced, produces evangelical repentance: Hence *Paul's* constant testimony both to *Jews* and *Greeks* was, *Repentance* toward God, and *faith* toward our Lord Jesus Christ, Acts 20:21. He first taught them their case before God, as breakers of his law, and then the way of reconciliation, by faith in Christ, who has fulfilled it; with which compare Mark 1:15. The Psalmist, when his heart was indicting good matter concerning *Zion's* King, describes this work in a very elegant manner, which is, that being armed with *truth*, meekness and righteousness, He in His majesty rides forth prosperously, and darts His arrows into His *enemies' hearts*; and all know that a wound there is death; accordingly they *fall under* Him; but how stout is the rebel that will fight till he dies! *Paul* can tell experimentally the nature of this death; it was death to his own *doings,* and the *hope* he built upon them, and he was *slain* thereto by the light: of this holy law, which discovered to him the *deceit* of his heart, which had operated in all his doings; Rom. 7:9-14; Phil. 3:4-9. These appear to the sinner *terrible things*; but how is the scene changed; when he sees the *sceptre of righteousness* presented from the *throne*, which gains the *enemy* to become the *Queen*; [alluding to Esther,ED.] most gloriously adorned! Thus are God's people *made willing* in the day of His *power*, to serve Him in the *beauty of holiness*, Psalms 45 and 110; Heb. 1:8-9.

I have been the more particular here to detect the deceit and blindness of the attempts that are often made, to **represent irresistible grace** to be *inconsistent* with the soul's liberty of choice; for here are descriptions of the work of grace that are absolutely irresistible, if any thing can be so; and yet there is not the least violence used with man's will, for the enemy is conquered with the full consent of all his heart: He is slain and made alive by the power of truth. And further to detect the delusion of many, and the false reasonings that are often used concerning sinners impotency, we will take a plain instance.

In the late rebellion in our nation, a hope of being *able* to usurp the throne, moved the rebels to invade *England*; but when they had marched within a hundred miles of *London*, that hope *failed* them, the effect of which was a hasty retreat back to *Scotland*; though by the way a hope of being *able* to keep the strong city of Carlisle against their Sovereign, caused them to leave a party in it for that purpose; but the Duke of *Cumberland* soon convinced them of their mistake, and then they hung out a sign; and upon his demanding its meaning; they said they wanted to *capitulate*. He replied, that he should enter into no *capitulation* with *rebels!* they should surrender to the King's mercy: They did accordingly. Now let us see where we are; it has been sufficiently proved that sinners are rebels against heaven, and that they will stand out in their rebellion till they are conquered; and if it would have been dishonorable to the King of *England* to have capitulated with these rebels, which yet were his fellow-men; what madness must it be to attempt to capitulate with rebels against the eternal God! What can all the noise mean concerning a day of grace, and good works for sinners to *do before* they are reconciled to the King of heaven, but only *inventions* of men to *keep off* from surrendering to Sovereignty, in hopes by and by to come in upon better terms! in hopes at last to be received, not as rebels, but subjects, who all along had a good regard for their King, and only happened to be imposed upon in some things. But be not deceived, God is not mocked; and all things are naked and opened to His eyes; all men's buildings which are not laid upon His precious *corner stone,* are nothing but *refuges of lies,* and God says, the *Hail shall sweep them away,* Psalm *28:15-17.*

As to power or ability; who need be told, that *in* nations, and *between* nations, the way to keep enemies from doing mischief, is to keep them sensible of their *inability* to do it? Even captives in the hands of savages whom they hate mortally, yet if they find they are *unable* to escape or to withstand them, they will be careful not to offend their cruel masters; how much more then will conviction, even in a carnal mind, that *it cannot* escape from, nor withstand a holy

God, restrain it and regulate its conduct? It is to this that we are indebted for much of the order and regulation in the world, which many falsely ascribe to men's good nature, and then turn it as an argument against the truth!

A sense of impotency has like effect upon the principle of *hope* as it has upon *fear;* as long as persons can hope to shift along themselves, they do not love to be dependent and beholden to others, but the clearer their sense is of being *unable* to do without others' help, the more earnest will be their cries there-for. "The *poor* useth *entreaties,* but the *rich* answereth *roughly*." The wicked through the *pride* of his countenance *will not seek after God,* Prov. *18:23;* Psalm *10:4.* How pernicious then are all those teachings that flatter the sinner's *pride,* by telling him of a great deal that he *can do,* and *must do,* in *order* to his coming to Christ! And as false and murderous to souls are all pretences that *impotency* can excuse any from their obligation this moment to *receive* God's *testimony,* and set to their *seal that He is true.* Many plead *impotency,* and pretend *honesty* in their restraining *prayer* before God; but they prove themselves *liars* in these very pretences; for profane mariners, who often pretend *honesty* in not seeking to God, because they *cannot* do it aright, yet when once they are brought to their *wits end* and find they *cannot* deliver themselves, *Then they cry unto him,* Psalm 107:27-28. Even an heathen ship-master could with astonishment ask Jonah *what he meant* to neglect it at such a time! Jonah 1:6. Could they be *honest* in neglecting such things, when they saw no danger, and yet be constrained to practice them when eternity appeared near! No; a deceived heart, and a deceiving devil, has turned them aside, to hold the truth in unrighteousness.

A rational soul is always governed in its choice, by the present ideas it has of what is best, let those ideas be true or delusive. Those who fall into the hands of savages, if they judge it best not to submit, they will choose to sell their lives as dear as they can; but if they judge it best to submit, then they will choose to be on as good terms with them as they can: And says Dr. *Owen*, "To suppose, that in all things of a spiritual and eternal concernment, that men are not determined and actuated every one by his own judgment, is an imagination of men who think but little of what they are, or do, or say, or write. Even those who *shut their eyes* against the light, and follow in the herd, *resolving* not to enquire into any of these things, do it, because they *judge it best for them so to do* (NOTE: Dr. *Owen's* Guide to Fellowship, page 74.)." Hence sin is called the works of *darkness*; and Satan's kingdom, the kingdom of *darkness*; and the way he has to keep any rational souls therein is, by *blinding* the minds of them that *"Believe not, lest the light of the glorious gospel should shine unto them"*: Yea, and they concur with him, for their *"ears are dull of hearing, and their eyes have THEY CLOSED, lest they should see, hear, understand,* and be *converted,* 2nd Cor. 4:4; *Acts 28:27.* It was only by *this ignorance* that the murderous *Jews* got along in their acting against Jesus; for had they *"Known Him, they would not have crucified the Lord of glory, 1st Cor. 2:8.*

One grand scheme of the learned free-willers of our day, to blind their own and others minds against these truths, is, to assert a self-determing power *in* the will, a power to act with motive, or against motive, just as the will pleases; but how little are such men aware, that they in this point *approve* of the deed of father *Adam,* at the same time that they deny their concern in it? The serpent proposed it as grand enlargement of our first parents *liberty,* that they should *Know both good and evil;* should be *free* to both; and he pretended that this was to be *as Gods;* they ventured to try the experiment, ventured to act against good motive, in order to be free to act either way as they pleased afterwards; but they found by sad experience that the serpent *lied* in this proposal.

With reverence be it spoken, the eternal God never had, nor never can have, such a liberty as these men tell of; for it is *impossible* for him to *lie,* and he *cannot be* so much as *tempted with evil,* Heb. 6:18; Jam. 1:13. These men's learned master *Locke* tells them plainly what they are doing: Says he, "Is it worth the name of *freedom* to be at *liberty* to play the fool, and draw shame and misery upon a man's self? If to break loose from the conduct of reason, and to want examination and judgment, which keep us from choosing or doing the worse, be true liberty, mad-men and fools are the only freemen; but yet I think nobody would choose to be Made for the sake of such liberty, but he that is mad already! (NOTE: Essay upon Understanding, B. 11, Chap. 21, page 50.)." And he goes on to observe, that, "As the highest perfection of intellectual nature, lies in a careful and constant pursuit of true and solid happiness; so the care of ourselves that we mistake not imaginary for real happiness, is the necessary foundation of our liberty, and the stronger ties we have to an unalterable pursuit of happiness in general, which is our greatest good, and which as such our desires always follow, the more are we free from any necessary determination of our *will* to any particular action, or from a necessary compliance with our desire, set upon any particular, and then appearing greater good, *till* we have duly examined whether it has a tendency to, or be inconsistent with our *real* happiness. ---I desire it may be well considered, whether the great inlet, and exercise of all the liberty men have, are capable of, or can be useful to them, and that whereupon depends the turn of their actions, does not lie in this, that they can suspend their desires, and stop them from determining their *wills* to any action, till they have duly and fairly examined the good and evil of it, as far forth as the weight of the thing requires (NOTE: *Ibid* pages 51, 52.)."

Thus far this great reasoner has followed the clear line of truth, yet in the next words he turns into the dark way, by saying "This we can do." If he had said, we can do it when we are assisted with divine light and truth, he had said well; but without such a proviso the matter is left in dark, because evil imaginations and desires have already got the start of reason, so that it can never bring them back to a fair examination without divine influence. Who is there that need be told, that if the judge is previously *biased*, we are not like to have a fair trial before him? Yet we are all so in this case; for a fair examination will certainly show that *self* is guilty; and if only a *gift* from *another* will *blind* the eyes of the wise, and *pervert* the words of the *righteous*; how much more will the honor, ease, yea life of *self*, blind the eyes of *sinners*, and hold them from a fair consideration of this case? For as God is the only fountain of all good, unbiased reason cannot but determine that every rational soul who loves and pursues any thing whatsoever as good, separate from, and in neglect of Him, is certainly guilty; yet that is what we have *all* done, though all do not pursue it in the same course, for we have turned every one to *his own way*, Isaiah 53:6. But who ever heard a judge give in a sentence, the immediate effect of which would bring himself from the bench to the bar, as a guilty prisoner? Since therefore reason is already biased, divine revelation is erected as the tribunal to decide this controversy: And wherever it truly takes place, it produces the effect just now mentioned; a notable instance of which we have recorded, Acts 24:24-25. A *Roman* governor and judge had the curiosity to send for his prisoner to hear him concerning the *faith in Christ*; but as the prisoner addressed the *reason* of the judge, concerning righteousness, temperance, and a judgment to come, the scene was remarkably changed for the *Roman* judge instantly becomes a *trembling* prisoner, while the prisoner is the King's officer to summon him to answer for his conduct at the awful bar. This was so disagreeable that he *put off* any further hearing for *that time*, and we have no grounds to think that the *convenient season* he flattered himself with ever came; and if not, then he is now a *spirit in prison*; while the record of his case stands for a warning to all others against the like *disobedience*, while the long-suffering of God waits with them, 1st Pet. 3:19-20.

But alas! instead of taking warning, we all naturally have the lawyer's disposition, who was willing to *justify himself*; his mind was biased that way: But how could he do it? Why he leaves God out of the question, and says, *Who is my neighbor*? This is a notable way to try rebels! for the judge to leave the King out of the question, and only examine their behavior to each other! Yet how poorly does he make out even in this way? For though they esteemed themselves so much better than the *Samaritans*, that they would have *no dealings* with them, yet our Lord sets before him a case in their own country, between *Jerusalem* and *Jericho*, which *Jewish* writers say, was then a station for priests and *Levites* (NOTE: See Dr. *Gill* on the place.), of one of each of those high characters who could *look* upon one whose case loudly called for their *compassion*, without being moved with it; but a *Samaritan* really acted the *neighbour* in the case, as the lawyer was forced to acknowledge: Jesus says, *Go and do thou likewise,* Luke 10:29-37.Note by the way, He does not say of this branch as He does of the whole law, "This do and thou shalt live;" no, yet He expressly shows, that this is binding on us all to be done, while the other is not to be left undone. This condemns all those who would either abate the law to bring it down to our ability, or in the least turn off its authority, and their obligation always to obey it, because of their inability.

However, though the attempt has often been made to justify self by leaving God out of the question, yet no rational person could ever entirely erase out of his mind an apprehension of a deity; therefore the common way, ever since man contracted a dislike to the true God, has been to make false ones to suit their own turn. When *Israel* rejected their true King, they made them *Idols according to their own understanding*, Hos. 13:2, 10, and so it is now. Some make up a deity in their minds, so fond of devotion, as to accept them for good worshipers, although they secretly grind the faces of the poor, and shut their hearts and hands against the needy. Others, viewing that way to be odious, frame an imagination of one who cares little for devotion, if men are but honest and kind to their neighbors. Though a third sort, not choosing to be under either of these restraints, frame a god that loves liberty, and their tongues would set him so high as not to concern himself with the conduct of worms, but leave them to gratify their own inclinations, provided they do but act as good fellows with each other; yet after all their great *swelling words*, they make their airy deity to be such an one as they scorn to be themselves, even such a *jack-at-a-pinch,* that whenever they find that they cannot indulge themselves any longer here, He shall be ready at their call, and take them directly to Paradise!

Oh! when will *brutish* and *foolish* man be *wise*! He that planted the ear, shall He not hear? He that formed the eye, shall He not see? He that chastiseth the *heathen*, shall not He correct? Yes verily, for He knoweth that the *thoughts* of man are *vanity*, Psalm 94:1-11.

From what has been proved, I appeal to every conscience whether the following conclusions are not certain truth:

I.   That all the love and good behavior that we can possibly have to our fellow-creatures, while our hearts are not truly united to our Creator, want the nature of true obedience, as much as the love and good order that may be in an army of rebels, wants of true obedience to their lawful Sovereign, when they are not reconciled to him.

II.   The reason why all men do not judge it to be so, is, because their *understandings* are *darkened* by an *alienation* and *bias* the other way, Eph. 4:18. Therefore,

III. For them to set up their reason against divine revelation, either to exclude any part of it, or to turn it aside from its plain genuine meaning, is as criminal as it can be for a *biased* judge to assume a power to *dispense* with any of the King's laws, or by false glosses and false evidences to *pervert* them from their just design, in order to acquit the guilty, or to condemn the innocent.

IV. All reasonings for an abatement of the law, or for the neglect of present obedience to it, because of our impotency, are pleas for the worst kind of treason and robbery; for God is infinitely lovely, and deserving of all our love, worship and obedience, and the only reason why we cannot yield Him all, is, because we do not *"Like to retain Him in our knowledge"*, but *love* and serve the *creature* instead of the *Creator*; one setting up *gain*, and another his *belly*, in God's place, thus *robbing* Him of His right, Rom. 1:24, 27; 1st Tim. 6:5; Phil. 3:19; Matt. 3:7-9.

V. All pleas against surrendering this momentto divine sovereignty, and receiving His proclamation of mercy in the gospel with all our hearts, are nothing but pleas still to adhere to the devil against the eternal God! They often say they cannot believe; but the only way that they have to keep from believing, is to shut their eyes and ears against the light and evidence of *truth*, and to join with the prince of darkness and his instruments to try to set up *falsehood* in its stead. They pretend to inquire for evidence of the truth of God's *promise,* while they are *willingly ignorant* that all things in *heaven* and *earth* have evidenced the power and truth of His *word* from the beginning, and will do so to *the day* of *judgment, and perdition of ungodly men,* 2nd Pet. 3:4-7. All pleas for not believing the gospel, are pleas to *make God a liar,* and to adhere to the *father of lies* instead of him, 1st John 3:8, 10.

VI.   Therefore it is perfectly *consistent* for Him plainly to set life and death before all men by the ministry of His word, and call them all to *turn and live*; although He does not intend to exert His almighty power to save any other than those that He has given to His Son, John 6:37 and John 17:2.

VII.   To make the doctrine of God's secret decrees any objection or excuse against a present and constant regard to His revealed will, is nothing less than to deny either His ability or His right to govern us; for it is essential to good government, to have a plan laid by the ruler, as well as rules given to the subjects, to which each should adhere in its place; and must not unbiased reason give in, that the more complete the plan is, and the less need of alteration, the better? And should you hear a person say, 'If I thought it was not in my power to penetrate into the King's secrets, or to *alter* his counsels, I would never pretend to obey his laws,' would you think him to be a subject or a rebel! Yet what can men's objections against the *unalterable* nature of the divine decrees, mean less than this? It is essential to moral government, that laws and rules should be given to men in a conditional form, enforced with the consideration of the rewards of obedience, and punishments of disobedience: And the just ruler will ever keep thereto in his administrations; but that is so far from excluding a secret plan, that it necessarily implies such an one; it implies, that as far as the ruler's wisdom and power can reach, he will be provided for all that shall happen, so as to be ready to do himself and his subjects justice, and not to be disappointed, nor lose his or their rights in any instance.

I suppose the art of man cannot set the *Arminian* notion of grace in a fairer light than this, viz., our late king, after the most criminal rebels were executed, pardoned others, and yet put them upon the trial of some difficult service for a time; before he confirmed their estates and privileges to them; so that their future welfare was *suspended* upon their doings. But then you must know, that as he had neither atonement for their crimes, nor power to change their hearts, if he had pardoned the chief rebels, it would have endangered the peace of the kingdom, if not his own crown, and there was reason for holding others in suspense, because he did not know their hearts, nor what their future conduct would be; and do men worship such a God as that! Again, law and justice require that each one has his due, but many involve themselves so as not to be able to pay their debts, and rather than lose all, many creditors will take up with a little part of their just due, and forgive the rest; and some, in hope of future gain, will trust the same persons again. This agrees with *Arminian* notions. But a few years ago there was an act made which emboldened a number of villains to launch out and get as much as they could of others' estates into their hands, in hopes of being rescued from justice by this pretended act of grace. This is like the *Antinomians*: Both of them would set up mercy to the injury of justice and truth, instead of meeting God at the true mercy-seat, where they agree and kiss each other. Both are for keeping off, one in hopes of compounding, or else of paying his debts with counterfeit money; the other to indulge himself as long as he can, with hopes at last to escape justice by pleading the bankrupt-act.

But let not men thus delude themselves, our eternal King is a *just God*, as well as a Saviour, Isaiah 14:21, and He will see that justice is done through the universe, and every soul shall be either brought to a reckoning here, and receive a clear discharge by our glorious Surety, yea and *quickly* too; or else be cast into that *prison* from whence they can by no means come out till they have paid the *uttermost farthing*, Matt. 5:25-26. And there is not a sinner upon earth that believes his debts to be so great as they are, nor that they are strictly just, till they are brought to a fair reckoning by the Spirit of truth; and 'tis well known, that if a creditor should cancel a debt, and the debtor still thought that it was unjustly charged, he could not heartily love him for it; therefore God brings every debtor, let him owe five hundred pence, or but fifty, to know that He is just, and that they have *nothing to pay, when He frankly forgives them*, Luke 7:42. And those who are forgiven, are so far from desiring to be trusted again with a stock in their own hands, that they durst not trust themselves; they desire ever to *trust in the Lord* with all their hearts, and not so much as *lean to their own understandings*, Prov. 3:5-6.

And now, kind reader, where is the absurdity and inconsistency of this plan? To hold that we have destroyed ourselves, and that all our help is in a sovereign God, who of his *own will* begets souls with the *word of truth*, and therefore calls us to *lay apart* every thing that tends to hinder our receiving it *understandingly* and *heartily*, and to watch against the devil's arts to *catch it away*, Jam. 1:18-21; Matt. 13:19-23. And are not those Satan's instruments, who use their art either to keep people from coming to hear the word, or to arm them against regarding it when they do come! Surely they are, therefore beware of them, as you regard your immortal souls. One of their most artful snares is to insinuate, that earnest addresses to men's minds betoken pride in the speaker; but though pride often operates in teachers as well as hearers, yet as it is exalting self, two of its never-failing fruits are deceit and bitterness; a deceitful handling of the word to suit their own ends, and bitterness if they are crossed therein, Prov. 13:10; Mic. 3:5, while humility, which exalts the Saviour, and abases self, ever produces faithfulness and love, and moves the preacher to renounce dishonesty, and a deceitful handling of the word, by manifestation of the truth to commend himself to every man's conscience in the sight of God, 2nd Cor. 4:2. But *Ahab* owned plainly that he *hated* such a preacher, and would allow him no better lodgings than a *prison*, nor better fare than *bread* and *water* of *affliction*, while he was willing delicately to maintain four hundred flatterers, though they soon lead him on to ruin, 1st Kings, 22:6-35. And alas! how much is there at this day of the same temper in the world, that had rather maintain four hundred flatterers than one faithful dealer!

The apostle *Jude*, in describing those who turn grace into lasciviousness, says, Wo unto them, for they have gone in the way of *Cain*, who because his doings were not accepted, was *very wroth*, and turned away to the noisy world; after which, like *Balaam*, they run *greedily*, who counselled *Balak* to lay a snare to draw *Israel* into sin; and to guard against conviction, they, like *Core*, accuse God's faithful servants with *taking too much* upon them, and with *lifting up themselves*. And given in what they know naturally, as *brute beasts*, they *corrupt themselves*; for who ever knew a beast take pains to blind his eyes, that he might not see a pit till he got into it! Who ever knew a bird labour hard to cover a net, so that she and her companions might not see their danger till they were taken and destroyed! Yet such is these men's conduct! Prov. 1:17-18; Jude 10:11.

To conclude, since precept and promise are united and ever go together in the gospel plan, in vain do men attempt to separate them: Every soul that truly believes the gospel, has with *Jacob* got what God *has said*, both to direct his conduct and to support him therein; and as truth declares, that *If any man will do, he shall know*, John 7:17, therefore all the attempts that are made by those who would be accounted believers, to excuse themselves from openly professing Christ, or to excuse their neglect of a faithful discharge of the duties of a member of His church, either from the plea of ignorance or inability, are nothing better than attempts to justify self, at the expense of God's honor! For as surely as He is true, He will never fail both to direct and support every one who trusts in Him, and is willing to obey Him. Then let none deceive themselves with the notion of being faints, if their hearts and lives are not governed and supported by truth; and if we are so, it will move us to a conscientious use of all the means which God has appointed, both of a public and private nature, to learn, and to promote truth in the world, and to avoid and watch against all that is contrary thereto.

APPENDIX

Containing a brief Account of the Sentiments of the first Baptist Churches in New England

IT is a just observation of an excellent writer, that ancient custom and modern fashion are two tyrants, which share the empire of the world between them; the truth of which often appears, both in civil and religious affairs. The name of the *good old way*, seems enough to prejudice many against the least variation from the customs of their fathers, and so against reformation; while others are so fond of novelties, as to be easily carried about with *every wind of doctrine*, that comes under a new and specious name, with exclamations against old *traditions* And though believers will regard the truth when they find it, for its own sake, yet it adds to their comfort to meet with others who know the same, which comfort is increased when they can commune with those who have lived long before them: Therefore having lately met with some things concerning the fathers of this country, which serve to confirm the foregoing discourse, and also to correct the mistakes of many, both in our denomination, and that are opposite thereto, who imagine that this doctrine was in ancient days peculiar to the Pedobaptists, I think it proper to insert a sketch thereof here. The oldest Baptist church in this land is at *Providence,* which was planted under the conduct of Mr. *Roger Williams;* and we may well conclude, that those who followed him into the great dangers and hardships of his exile, had a good liking to the doctrines which he taught, and what they were we may gather from the various accounts we have of him.

He came first to this country on *February 5, 1631,* being in his youth, and he preached a while at *Salem,* but the Court of Assistants at *Boston* wrote to the church against him the 12th of *April* following, which prevented their calling him to office then, and he went to *Plymouth,* where he preached about three years; and Governor *Winthrop,* and Mr. *Wilson,* of *Boston,* upon *a* visit there, communed with him at the Lord's supper, on *October* 28, 1632 (NOTE: Mr. *Prince's* Annals, vol. 2, p. 26, 47, 70.). He removed back again to *Salem,* and taught them there in the time of Mr. *Skelton's* sickness, and after his death, which happened *August* 2, 1634 (NOTE: Magnalia, b. 3, P. 76.), Mr. *Williams* was ordained over that church; but such difference arose, that he was banished out of the colony the same year, and he and a few friends that followed him settled at *Providence,* where they soon after embraced the Baptist principles. And though to justify or excuse the severity that was used against him, a great deal has been written to render him odious and ridiculous, yet Dr. *Mather,* after much of that nature, says, "It was more than forty years after his exile that he lived here (at *Providence*) and in many things acquitted himself so laudably, that many judicious persons judged him to have had the *root of the matter* in him. ---He used many commendable endeavours to Christianize the *Indians* in his neighbourhood, of whose language, tempers and manners, he has printed a little relation.—There was also a good correspondence always held between him and many worthy and pious people in the colony from whence he had been banished. ---Against the Quakers, he afterward maintained the main principles of the *Protestant religion* with much vigour (NOTE: Magnalia, b. 3, p. 9)." His endeavours to Christianize the Indians appear to be the first that were used by any in this country, for we are told that the famous Mr. *Eliot* preached his first sermon to them in the year 1646 (NOTE: Ibid. p. 196.); whereas Mr. *Williams* went to *England* in 1642, and obtained a charter from the ruling powers there, which is dated March 14, 1643 (NOTE: See a copy of the charter in the *Providence Gazette,* No. 121, February 9, 1765.), and with it a letter to the authority in the Massachusetts, wherein they begin thus: "Taking notice some of us of long time of *Roger Williams*, his good affections and conscience, and of his sufferings by our common enemy, and oppressors of God's people, the prelates, as also of his great industry and travels in his printed *Indian* labours in your parts (the like whereof we have not seen extant from any part of *America*) and in which respect it hath pleased both Houses of Parliament to grant unto him, and friends with him, a free and absolute charter of civil government (NOTE: *Massachusetts* History, vol. I, p. 39.)," etc., from whence we may well conclude that he was early in his endeavours, since he had got furnished so as to print a relation of their language and manners before that time. And though after gathering a Baptist church at *Providence,* Mr. *Williams's* mind got so blundered, with the notion that many try to propagate to this day, of the necessity of a local succession from the apostles to empower persons to administer ordinances, and not being able to give in to the absurdity of deriving this power through the long scene of antichristian corruption, that he desisted from traveling with that church, yet the church has continued to this day; and Mr. *Williams* always discovered a respect for them, and sundry times expresses the same in his book concerning the Quakers, wherein he at one time mentions *Thomas Olney*, at another time, *Pardon Tillinghast*, whom he stiles "Able and leading men among the people called Baptists in *Providence*," p. 142, and 208. And even in the midst of Dr. *Mather's* talk of their dissolution, he says they *kept* to this one principle, "That every one should have liberty to worship God according to the light of his own conscience (NOTE: Magnalia, b. 3, p. 9);" which implies continuance of worship among them; and they appear to be the first civil government that ever allowed and acted upon this principle in all the Protestant world; and whether they deserve reproach for it, and others honour for denying them that liberty, let the reader judge!

A late historian of high rank, speaking of Mr. *Williams*, says, "After all that has been said of the actions or tenets of this person while he was in the *Massachusetts*, it ought for ever to be remembered to his honour, that for forty years after, instead of showing any revengeful resentment against the colony, from which he had been banished, he seems to have been constantly employed in acts of kindness and benevolence, giving them notice from time to time, not only of every motion of the *Indians*, over whom he had a very great influence, but also of the unjust designs of the *English* within the new colony, of which he himself had been the founder and Governor, and continued the patron (NOTE: *Massachusetts* History, vol. I, p. 38.)." And as to his teaching, Governor *Bradford*, one of the most eminent fathers of *Plymouth*, writes thus: "Mr. *Roger Williams* (a man godly and zealous, having many precious parts, but very unsettled in judgment) came over first to the *Massachusetts*; but upon some discontent left the place and came hither, where he was freely entertained, according to our poor ability, and exercised his gifts, and after some time was admitted a member of the church, and his teaching well approved; for the benefit whereof I still bless God, and am thankful to him even for his sharpest admonitions and reproofs, so far as they sharpest agreed with truth (NOTE: *Prince's* Annals, vol. 2, p. 48.)." Now it is well known, that those fathers of *Plymouth*, who *well approved* of Mr. *Williams's* teaching, held fully to the **absolute sovereignty of grace**; and Mr. *Callender*, after informing us of a division which arose in the church at *Providence* about the year 1653, concerning laying on of hands, says, "That church which was distinguished by holding *laying on of hands, necessary* to all baptized persons, came in time generally to hold *universal redemption;"* which he observes, was a departing from some of Mr. *Williams's* "Darling opinions (NOTE: Mr. *Callender's* century sermon, p. 61.)." This alteration from their first principles, it seems, came in gradually about twenty years after their first settlement at *Providence*.

The second Baptist church in *New England* was gathered at *Newport*, under the care of Mr. *John Clark*, about the year 1644; and what their faith was you may see a little of in the following extracts: "The decree of God is that whereby God hath from eternity set down with Himself whatsoever shall come to pass in time, Eph. 1:11. All things with their causes, effects, circumstances, and manner of being, are decreed by God, Acts 2:23. Him being delivered by the *determinate counsel* and foreknowledge of God, etc., Acts 4:28. This decree is most wise, Rom. 11:33, ---Most just, Rom. 9:13-14, ---Eternal, Eph. 1:4-5; 2nd Thes. 2:13, ---Necessary, Psalm 33:11, Prov. 19:21, ---Unchangeable, Heb. 6:17, ---Most free, Rom. 9:18, ---And the cause of all good, James 1:17, ---But not of any sin, 1st John 1:5.

The special decree of God concerning angels and men is called *predestination*, Rom. 8:30, of the former, viz., angels, little is spoken in the holy scripture; of the latter more is revealed, not unprofitable to be known. It may be defined, "The wise, free, just, eternal, and unchangeable sentence, or decree of God, Eph. 1:11, determining to create and govern man for His special glory, viz. the praise of His glorious mercy and justice," Rom. 9:17-18 and 11:36.

Election is the decree of God, of His free love, grace and mercy, choosing some men to faith, holiness, and eternal life; for the praise of His glorious mercy, 1st Thes. 1:4; 2nd Thes. 2:13; Rom. 8:29-30. The cause which moved the Lord to elect them who are chosen, was none other but His mere good will and pleasure, Luke 12:32; Rom. 11:5, 9, 11, 16; Eph. 1:5; 2nd Tim. 1:9. The end is the manifestation of the riches of His grace and mercy, Rom. 9:23; Eph. 1:6. The sending of Christ, faith, holiness and eternal life, are the effects of His love, by which He manifesteth the infinite riches of His grace, John 3:16; Acts 8:48; Rom. 6:23, in the same order God doth execute this decree in time, He did decree it in His eternal counsel, 1st Thes. 5:9; 2nd Thes. 2:13. Sin is the effect of man's free will, and condemnation is an effect of justice inflicted upon man for sin and disobedience, John 3:18 and 12:37. A man in this life may be sure of this election, 2nd Peter 1:10; 1st Thes. 1:4. Yea of His eternal happiness, Matt. 24:24; John 10:28-29. But not of His eternal reprobation, for He that is now profane, may be called hereafter, Matt. 20:5-6." These extracts I carefully took from what Mr. *John Comer* recorded with his own hand, while he was pastor of that church, which he prefaced with these words: viz. "Having found in the hands of brother *Edward Smith* a small book, written by Mr. *John Clark,* the first pastor of this church, containing his judgment, and the judgment of the church, respecting that soul-supporting doctrine of *personal election,* which is at this day so much contemned; for the establishing the church under its present constitution in this glorious truth, I think it not improper to transcribe it, this 31st day of July, 1727."

Here note, these were both the sentiments of Mr. *Clark* and of his church, of which he continued the pastor till his death, which happened on April 20, 1675, only as his sufferings in the *Massachusetts* occasioned his going to *England*, where he procured the present *Rhode Island* charter.

Therefore since Mr. *Williams*, who procured their first charter from the Parliament, and Mr. *Clark*, who obtained their present charter from the King, and the two first churches in the colony, were so full in this **doctrine of sovereign grace**, how illy does it become any inhabitant of that colony now to exclaim against the doctrine as an old notion of other sects, but as what was new among them? And how unjust has it been in many others, to represent the contrary doctrine as peculiarly belonging to the Baptists (NOTE: Mr. *Callender* informs us, that the doctrine of *free will* and *laying on of hands* caused a separation in the church of *Newport*, about the same time of that at *Providence*, Century sermon, p. 65. And Governor *Joseph Jenckens*, speaking in a letter to a friend, dated March 19, 1730, of the opinion that laying on of hands ought not to be any bar of communion with those who have been rightly baptized, says, "I have been informed by one, or more, of the ancient members of our church at *Providence*, that such was the opinion of the Baptists in the first constitution of their churches throughout this colony.")?

For as that was not the case in the two first of their churches in this country, so neither was it with the third, which is the first in the *Massachusetts* province, namely that of *Swanzey*. I find by the records of that church, that it was constituted in the year 1649, at *Ilston*, in *Glamorganshire, South Wales*, where it prospered under the ministry of Mr. *John Miles*, till he was ejected from thence by the act of uniformity, which turned so many godly men out of their places in 1662 (NOTE: Dr. *Calamy's* account of ejected ministers, vol. 2, p. 731.); after which, he and a considerable part of his church came over and settled at *Swanzey*, which was then in *Plymouth* Colony, who were more moderate towards dissenters than some were; hence in Dr. *Mather's* account of that colony he says, "There has been among them one church, that questioned and omitted the use of infant baptism; nevertheless, there being many good men among those of that persuasion, I do not know that they have been *persecuted*, with any harder means, than those of kind conferences to reclaim them (NOTE: Magnalia, b. I, p. 14.)." And speaking of ministers that he could not tell how to put among their *worthies*, he says, "I confess, there were some of those persons, whose names deserve to live in our book for their *piety*, although their peculiar opinions were such, as to be disserviceable unto the declared and supposed interests of our churches.[Congregationalists –ED] Of these there were some godly Anabaptists; as namely, Mr. *Hanfard Knollys*, of *Dover*, who afterwards removing back to *London*, died there, *a good man, in a good old age*. And Mr. *Miles*, of *Swanzey*, who afterwards came to *Boston* (NOTE: Though he might labour a while at *Boston*, yet I am told that he died among his own people of *Swanzey*.), and is now gone to his rest. Both of these have a respectful character in the churches of this wilderness (NOTE: Book 3, p.7.)." And Mr. *Hutchinson* says, I have seen a letter from Mr. *Miles*, the Baptist minister at *Swanzey*, to one of the congregational ministers at *Boston*, which breaths the true spirit of the gospel, and urges Christian concord, charity and love, although they did not agree in every point (NOTE: *Massachusetts* History, vol. I, p. 228.)." Once more, as Mr. *Clark* and his church held election to be God's choosing some men **TO** faith, holiness, and eternal life, for the praise of His glorious mercy, and that, "The cause which moved the Lord to elect them who are chosen, was *none other* but His mere good will and pleasure," which He executes in the *same order* in time; and as Mr. *Comer* call this a *glorious truth*, and a *soul-supporting* doctrine; so his preaching this gospel at *Rehoboth*, in the year 1731, was the powerful means of converting many souls, whom Mr. *Comer* baptized, and so gathered the first Baptist church there, of which the late Elder *Richard Round* was one, who with others held this doctrine to the last. Therefore as I think

I have proved that Mr. *Martin*, (who belongs to another society in that town) has acted against Scripture and reason, in denying this doctrine; so he also has against the testimony of his pious fathers; yea I may add, of his fathers in the other *England* as well as this; for the first confession of faith which was published by the *English* Baptists, was published by seven churches in *London*, in 1643 (NOTE: This was some years before the *Westminister* confession or catechism.), wherein they as fully express their belief of **absolute sovereignty in election**, as Messeurs *Clark* or *Comer* do, and they say, "Faith is the gift of God, wrought in the - - hearts of the elect by the Spirit of God; by which faith they come to know and believe the truth of the Scriptures, and the excellency of them, above all other writings, and all things in the world, as they hold forth the glory of God in His attributes, the excellency of Christ in His nature and offices, and of the power and fullness of the Spirit in its workings and operation, and so are enabled to cast their souls upon this truth thus believed. ---Faith is ordinarily begotten by the preaching of the gospel, or word of Christ, without respect to any power or agency in the creature; but it being wholly passive, and dead in trespasses and sins, doth believe and is converted by *no less power than that which raised Christ from the dead* (NOTE: *Crosby's* History of *English* Baptists, vol. I, appendix, p. 15, 16.)." Two of the many texts which they cite to prove these articles, are John 6:63; Eph. 1:19.

I am far from desiring any to follow the most eminent fathers any further than they followed Christ; but as I fully believe that these fathers did so, in the **doctrine of sovereign grace,** in *overcoming evil with good*, and in maintaining a friendly correspondence with pious people of other denominations, while they still kept to this one principle, for each one to worship God according to the light of his own conscience; who can justly blame this attempt to promote these generous principles, which I would thankfully acknowledge are of late, in a considerable measure, revived in their children?

F I N I S

ELECTION, PERSEVERANCE, AND GOD'S DECREES
by
Isaac Backus, 1789

[John Wesley wrote a stunning attack against Augustus Toplady and the doctrine of election and predestination, and the doctrine held by the supralapsarian Calvinists. Toplady, John Gill, and Issac Backus answered his heretical blasphemy. This is Backus' reply,]

Controversy is generally complained of and peace is earnestly sought, but often in a way that denies to all others the liberties we claim for ourselves. The revealed will of God is the only perfect law of liberty, but how little is it believed and obeyed by mankind. Both the Hebrew and Christian churches were to be wholly governed by it, and when the first king of Israel presumed to violate a plain command of God, and then thought to atone for it by acts of worship, he was guilty of rebellion, which is as the sin of witchcraft, (1 Sam. 15:23.) And in like way Mystery Babylon by her sorceries has deceived all nations, and in her was found the blood of prophets, and of saints, and of all that were slain upon the earth. (Rev. 18: 23-24.) Yet these extensive terms are so limited by carnal reasoners that none of them, in any nation, will admit themselves to be of that bloody city. And at the same time they are for extending general words of grace beyond any limits and are ready to accuse us with making God deceitful if we hold that He did not design the merits of His Son equally for all mankind.

If we inquire then, why all are not saved, the general answer is that they would not receive that salvation, or if they did for awhile, and then turned away from it, God rejects and destroys them for it. We readily grant that God always rewards the righteous and never destroys any **for anything but sin** and iniquity, but this cannot content many without we will allow that grace has put power into the **wills** of all mankind to become righteous and to obtain salvation when they **shall be pleased** to set about it in earnest. The fruit of which is that men neglect the great salvation because they love darkness rather than light. *"Yea, everyone that doeth evil hateth the light."* (Heb. 2:3; John 3:19,20.) And when any are brought to obey the truth and so come to the light, every art is made use of to get them into darkness again if possible!

This has been remarkably the case in the southern parts of America. Many of their teachers were so dark as to swear profanely, drink to excess, and follow gaming and at the same time to preach up *do and live, work and be blessed,* to their people. But the light of the pure Gospel produced reformation among some of them about forty years ago (The Great Awakening period-ed.), and it has greatly increased since 1768, as I was well informed when I was called to travel and preach in Virginia and North Carolina last winter. But after this reformation had spread extensively, the followers of Mr. John Wesley introduced his writings against particular election and final perseverance and thereby greatly obstructed the work of truth. I was therefore requested to publish a brief answer thereto. His first piece on that subject was published above fifty years ago under the title of free grace, and it was closed with a hymn called "Universal Redemption," and therein Mr. Wesley says:

"Thine eye surveyed the fallen race,
When sunk in sin they law,
Their misery called for all thy grace,
But justice stopped the way.
Mercy the fatal bar removed,
Thy only son it gave,
To save a world so dearly loved,
.A sinful world to save.
For every man he tasted death,
He suffered once for all,
He calls as many souls as breathe,

And all may hear the call.
A power to choose, a will t' obey,
Freely his grace restores;
We all may find the living way,
And call the savior ours."

He denied that man had **any natural liberty of will left after the fall until it was restored by grace** [A few now held by most Conditional Primitive Baptists - Ed.]. This he more explicitly did in a pamphlet on Predestination, Election, and Reprobation published in 1776; and said upon it, "We believe, that in the moment Adam fell he had no freedom of will left; but that God, when of His own free grace He gave the promise of a Savior to him and his posterity, **graciously restored to mankind a liberty and power to accept of proffered salvation."** (page 16.) But if the fall took all natural liberty of choice from man until grace restored it, then the fall released him from the authority of the law of God as it was first given to him, and he never has been under it since, but by grace. The beasts are not under that law because they never had the powers of thinking and choice as rational creatures have, and if men are not under the law, what are they better than beasts? Yea, do they not corrupt themselves more than brute beasts that know and obey their owners? (Jude 10, Isa. 1:2-4.) And if all freedom of the will is from grace, then it is only by grace that any have the will or power to sin against God, as none can sin against Him who have no natural liberty of will! This opinion of Mr. Wesley's is most plainly confuted by the case of the fallen angels who never had any grace revealed to them. Yet the Devil sinneth from the beginning, and all willful sinners are *"children of the devil"* in opposition to all those who are "born of God" (John 3:8-10.) In the same book Mr Wesley says : "1. God's love was the **cause** of his sending His son to die for sinners. 2. Christ's dying for sinners is the **cause** of the gospel's being preached. 3. The preaching of the gospel is the **cause**, or means, of our believing. 4. Our believing is the **cause or condition** of our justification. 5. The knowing ourselves justified through his blood is the **cause** of our love of Christ. 6. Our love to Christ is the **cause** of our obedience to Him. 7. Our obedience to Christ is the **cause** of His becoming the author of eternal salvation to us. Page 8.

And is not this going about to establish our own righteousness? For Moses described the righteousness which is of the law, saying, *"That the man who doth those things, shall live by them."* This is a *"zeal of God but not* according *to knowledge"* (Rom. 10:2-5). Mr. Wesley goes on to say: "I shall now briefly show the dreadful absurdities that follow from saying "Christ died only for the elect." He said, "If Christ died not for all, then unbelief is no sin in them that finally perish, seeing there is not anything for those men to believe unto salvation for whom Christ died not. 2. If Christ died not for all men, then it would be a sin in the greatest part of mankind to believe He died for them, seeing it would be to believe a lie. 3. If Christ died not for those that are damned, then they are not damned for unbelief, otherwise you say, that they are damned for not believing a lie. [Publisher's comment: We agree with his argument in numbers 1, 2, and 3, for we ourselves do not believe it is required of the reprobate children of the Devil to believe Christ died for them, or to believe unto salvation, which they can't. We believe they are required only to believe what God has commanded them to believe, even in His eternal power and Godhead. Reprobates were not chosen in Him, are not now in Him, have never been in Him from the beginning of the foundation of the world, as the elect have been, and they shall never be in Him. Natural suasion or nominal belief will not put them in Him.]

4. If Christ died not for all, then those who

obey Christ by going and preaching the gospel to every creature as glad tidings of grace and peace, of great joy to all people, do sin thereby; in that they go to most people with a lie in their mouth. [Note: This is true of all Arminians and Pelagians, for they preach that He died for all, when in fact He died for His sheep only,] 5. If Christ died not for all men, then God is not in earnest in calling all men everywhere to repent, for what good could repentance do those for whom Christ died not? 6. If Christ died not for all, then why does He say, He is not willing that any should perish? Surely He is willing, yea, resolved that most men should perish, else He would have died for them also. 7. How shall God judge the world by the man Christ Jesus, if Christ did not die for the world or how shall He judge them according to the gospel when there was never any gospel or mercy for them? (Page 4.) –John Wesley's Quote closed.

ANSWER by Backus: If Christ died with a design to save all men, why are not all saved? Can the Devil cheat Him of a great part of His purchase? Or, can men defeat His merciful designs? No, say many, He died for all, and He will finally save all (Universalists, or Socinians.)

Others go farther and conclude that a God of infinite goodness could not give existence to any creature that shall be miserable without end, but that He will finally deliver every child of Adam from hell (Hell Redemptionists), though many of them will be tormented therein for ages of ages. But how is their deceit here discovered? Fallen angels were as really the creatures of God as fallen men, yet no salvation was ever revealed for them, but they are *"reserved in everlasting chains under darkness"* unto the judgment of the great day. And this is a clear evidence against ungodly men who *"turn the grace of God into lasciviousness."* (Jude 4, 6.) God was so far from ever proclaiming atonement to all men without exception, that He said, *"The soul that doth ought presumptuously, the same reproacheth the Lord and that soul shall be cut off from among His people."* And for such presumption, Korah and his company perished most terribly (Num. 15:30; 16: 1-3; 31-34.) For if the inability of men, as the scripture testify, or if as debtors and criminals could release them from the authority of the laws, until rulers would give them power to bring the government to their own terms, how would all dominion be despised! These *"filthy dreamers"* have now filled the world with Babylonian confusion. (Jude 8.) The Jews called it heresy in Paul to believe in and obey Jesus as a lawgiver above Moses. (Acts 24:14.)

And this is the first place where the word heresy is used in the Bible, and if we observe what is said in the last chapter in it of every man who shall add to or take from its words, we must conclude that all men who do so and violently impose their **inventions** upon others are guilty of heresy?

The head of the church of Rome assumed God's place in that assembly, and exalted himself above God, who never could violate His promise or His oath or entice any into sin, and how justly are all those given up to strong delusion who practice either of these evils? (2 Thess. 2: 3-12; Heb. 6:18; James 1: 13-15.) And how happy should we soon be if these iniquities were excluded from our land.

True believers are so far from presuming upon the secret designs of God that when the same are revealed, they dare not make His designs, but His laws, the rule of their conduct. Though His design of removing Saul and making David king over Israel was clearly revealed, yet David refused to kill Saul when greatly provoked thereto because he had no direction to do it. Neither did David assume regal power over Israel until each tribe freely received him as their king by a solemn covenant. But the envious Jews no sooner had it declared to them that Jesus was to die for that nation than from that day forth they took counsel together for to put Him to death. (John 11:53.) Hereby we may see the plain difference between true believers and reprobate believers. *"For unto the pure all things are pure, but unto the defiled and unbelieving is nothing pure, but even their mind and conscience is defiled. They profess that they know God, but in works they deny Him, being abominable, and disobedient, and unto every good work reprobate."* (Titus 1: 15,16.) In this way, teachers who turn grace into lasciviousness deny the only Lord God and our Lord Jesus Christ. (Jude 4.) But many are deceived by them because in words they profess to know Him. Since Christ was exalted to the right hand of the Father, His only priests upon earth are the *"elect according to the foreknowledge of God the Father, through sanctification of the Spirit unto obedience, and sprinkling of the blood of Jesus Christ. Being born again, not of corruptible seed, but incorruptible, by the Word of God which liveth and abideth forever.* These are the chosen generation, a royal priesthood, an holy nation, a peculiar people, that they should show forth the praise of Him who hath called them out of darkness into His marvelous light. (1 Pet. 1:2, 23; and 2:5,9.)

But Mr. Wesley, in his piece on predestination, election, and reprobation, says:

"They were chosen through belief of the truth and called to believe it by the Gospel; therefore they were not chosen before they believed, much less before they had a being." (Page 5.) And in his sermon from Romans 8:29, 30, he says: "God looking on all ages from the creation to the consummation as a moment and seeing at once whatever is in the hearts of all the children of men knows every one that does or does not believe in every age or nation. Yet what He knows, whether faith or unbelief, is no wise caused by His foreknowledge. Men are as free in believing or not in believing, as if He did not know it at all." (Page 6.)

I readily grant that His knowledge does not **cause any sin**, which is altogether in and **of the creature**. The angels who fell kept not the first estate but left their own habitation. (Jude 6.) And those who stood were elect angels. (1 Tim. 5:21.) And sin came into human nature **by violating a known command.** And Adam was a figure of Jesus Christ, and therefore death reigned over all his posterity, many of whom never committed any actual transgressions as he did. And the word "as" so often used in this affair, cannot be true in any sense if both Adam and Christ were not heads and representatives of **all the seed of**

each. It is certain that Adam was not a figure of Christ, as he conveyed death and ruin to his posterity by a just sentence of law; for Christ conveys life and salvation to souls by a **free gift** of grace. Neither could Adam be a figure of Christ in the great things that he did by one offence, *"for Christ atoned for many offences; therefore where sin abounded, grace did much more abound."* (Rom. 5:12-21.) I say the word "as" cannot be true in all these places unless those **two men acted for all their seed**. Many would have it, that this word cannot be true unless Christ atoned for as many as fell in Adam, but **certain** death came upon all Adam's race while multitudes hold that salvation by Christ is **uncertain** and depends upon the **natural wills** of individuals. In this view they would make Christ vastly inferior to Adam whose doings were efficacious, and the doings of Christ exceeding precarious, upon their plan. And they who hold that Christ will finally save all the race of Adam from hell, yet imagine that the creature's sufferings must save them and not the efficacy of the death and grace of Christ; or if they hold that He will save all from future sufferings, they hold also that He has now saved them from the authority of the law of God, which Adam never did. By the sentence of it every child of Adam returns to the dust, the righteous as well as the wicked, so that if the doings of Christ are not efficacious for the final salvation of His seed, it cannot truly be said that *"as in Adam all die, even so in Christ shall all be made alive."*

THE SOVEREIGN DECREES OF GOD
By
Isaac Backus, 1773

Beloved Friend,

Although we should endeavor to avoid all needless contention, yet the *"faith once delivered to the saints,"* is sometimes treated in such a manner as to make it our incumbent duty *earnestly* and publicly to *contend* for it. Such a case I think is presented before us by means of a printed paper lately spread in Providence, R.I., and towns adjacent which you have requested me to make some remarks upon. It begins in this manner:

"On Traditional Zeal: Some good Christian pastors will not scruple to tell you that they could find no joy in "their own state, no strength or comfort in their labors of love towards their flocks, but because they know and are assured from St. Paul that God never had, nor ever will have, mercy upon all men; but that an unknown multitude of them are, through all ages of the world, inevitably decreed to the eternal fire and damnation of hell; and that an unknown number of others are elected to a certain, irresistible salvation. Wonder not, my friends, if the inquisition has its pious defenders, for inquisition, cruelty, and every barbarity that must have an end, is mere mercy if compared with this **reprobation doctrine.** And to be in love with it, to draw comfort from it, and to wish it Godspeed is a love that absolutely forbids the loving our neighbors as our own selves and makes the Scripture-wish, that all men might be saved, no less than a rebellion against God." -End quotation.

This writer's evident design is against the doctrine of **particular election and efficacious grace** in our salvation, and against those who preach it. And he takes the same *"method"* that the heathen persecutors did with the Primitive Christians, *viz.*, to cover them with skins of wild beasts in order that they might be devoured by dogs, or if not, yet that they might be hated and avoided by all men. He asserts that some "Christian pastors" tell their people such a story as he has here related. If he can find any man upon earth that teaches so, he is welcome to correct him as much as he deserves, but till he exhibits his proof he ought to be accounted a blasphemer of God's Sovereignty and a false teacher of Christ's ministers. Yea, out of his own mouth he is condemned, for as short as his paper is he has not been able to keep to one consistent story, but the same preachers that he accuses of *rejoicing* that God never will have mercy upon all men, when he comes to give us their own language it is, *"O, the sweetness of God's election!"* And neither the Devil nor any of his children will ever be able to make a rejoicing in God's *everlasting love to a chosen number* to be the same thing as it would be to rejoice in the destruction of the rest.

Our Lord says, *"Every one that doth evil hateth the light, but he that doth truth cometh to the light"* (John 3:21); and let the reader judge which of these characters suits the conduct of the writer before us. He cast out these horrid accusations against some good Christian pastors without naming any one, while his evident aim is against **all** that profess a sweetness in sovereign election; at the same time (like savages) he tries to keep himself and his own principles hid. Though it fares with him as it did with the old enemies of the *sure foundation that God has laid in Zion,* whose bed was shorter than a man could stretch upon it, and the covering narrower than that he could wrap himself in it (Isaiah

28). For though by the title of his piece he would have people esteem him as a bold champion against *tradition* and a friend of Paul and the sacred writings, yet he does not so much as attempt to prove that **sovereign decrees and irresistible grace** are not fully taught by them. No, instead of confusing us or defending himself by the sacred oracles, he, like those who prophesied out of the *deceit in their own hearts,* first makes his address to men's passions and exerts all his art to bring up the horrid ideas of an inevitable decreeing of multitudes to hellfire, of cruelty vastly worse than the **inquisition,** of God's sacrificing of myriads of His creatures to the devil, *etc.,* and having done his utmost thus to raise a tempest in the souls of men, he winds up by asserting that "The only possible way of avoiding every prevailing error and of finding every saving truth is to listen, solemnly, attentively to listen, agreeable to the written word, to the *"still small voice within you."*

This is just like the old Serpent who, with malicious reflections upon God's government and lying pretences of friendship to man drew him into rebellion against God's ***revealed will*** and to gratify his own heart's lust. Yet from that day to this, when the tempter thinks it will serve his turn, he is very ready to catch at some portion of Scripture *words,* to entice people into violations of the *truth* which is therein taught.

Let the pretended advocate for the truth now before us mean what he will by the *voice within*, yet when he or any others are brought solemnly and attentively to listen either to reason, conscience, or the Spirit of God they will teach them that the way to avoid error and to find the truth in any case, is not first to inflame our passions before our judgments are well formed. No! for a *gift will blind the eyes of the wise and pervert the words of the righteous* (Deuteronomy 16:19); therefore we must have our eye single or else our *whole body will be full of darkness*. Hence appears the necessity of the Holy Spirit to renew us in the spirit of our minds and to guide our souls into all truth.

The grand contest ever since sin entered into the world has been between the **will of the Creator** and the **will of the creature.** But as it is too shocking for human nature to have it openly appear in that light, God's enemies in all ages have *"made lies their refuge and under falsehood have hid themselves"* (Isaiah 28:15). And in the controversy before us we may take notice of the following refuge of lies that the enemies *sovereign grace* try to hide themselves in.

First, As the sacred writers often appealed to men's reason and conscience and exhorted the saints to regard the teachings of the Holy Spirit in their souls above all human authority on earth, deceivers of various denominations have caught at and perverted that sacred custom as a place for setting up a standard *in themselves* to decide every case so as not to admit anything for truth that does not agree with their *inward imaginary test*. But it is well known in our nation that in order for us to enjoy our just rights and liberties, rulers as well as subjects must be **governed by known laws and established legal rules,** and for judges to assume a discretionary power to dispense with old laws or to make NEW ONES as occasion serve would introduce arbitrary government, or rather a CRUEL TYRANNY. And were not people deluded with the *religious names* and great swelling words of deceivers, as their attempts to set up a *voice within* that speaks in any respects contrary to God's **written Word** would appear as arbitrary and tyrannical as any such proceedings of earthly judges can be. Those holy men whom God employed to write His Word had their authority so to do *"with signs and wonders, and with divers miracles and gifts of the Holy Ghost, according to His own will"* (Hebrews 2:4) and woe to that man who presumes either to add to, or take from, those holy oracles.

Second: The advocates for their own **"free will"** in opposition to sovereign grace have determined that the doctrine of **eternal *fixed* decrees** in the Divine Mind concerning the future state of men, is consistent with the "liberty" of their own wills, and with proper influence of precepts and promises, rewards and punishments. And, having quoted a number of precepts with considerations to enforce them (of which the Bible is full) they boast that they have gained their argument, when in truth they have never even touched the point in debate! We know, and as firmly as any free willer on earth, that **all men are under *moral government*** where precepts and promises, exhortations, warnings, *etc.,* have their proper place, and ought to influence us in **all our conduct.** And I believe from the bottom of my heart that God never did or ever will punish any but the guilty, and that He will finally reward *"every man according to his works"* (Matthew 16:27). But in the present controversy the true state of the question is this, *viz.,* **Whether the whole plan of God's government and the final issue of *every action* throughout the universe has not been known and *fixed* in His counsel from the beginning, so that *"nothing can be put***

to it nor anything taken from it"
(Ecclesiastes 3:14), Or, whether *many events*
are not held in *suspense and uncertainty* in
His infinite Mind, till they are **decided by
"free will power"** of men? We hold the first,
they the last side of this question. But instead
of attending to the true state of the
controversy, and instead of referring the
decision of it to the Divine oracles, *tradition*
and *corruption* has carried them into the way
which this writer pursues of representing our
doctrine to be that God decrees some to
misery in the same manner that He does
others to happiness. Yea, this slanderer, in
imitation of those who have gone before him,
sets **reprobation** foremost and would have
people believe that we hold God's ***first*** design
to be the damnation of "multitudes" and then,
secondly, the "irresistible salvation of a
number"! Hoping no doubt by these horrid
colorings to guard people sufficiently against
all the Gospel weapons that are appointed to
pull down the strongholds that are raised
against the knowledge of God, and to cast
down the *imaginations* which keep men's
thoughts *too high* to yield their all to a meek
and lowly Jesus (II Corinthians 10: 4,5). Many
in latter ages have carried their imaginations
so high on this subject as to:

Third. To assume a dignity to themselves that they will not allow in the Eternal God, for they claim for themselves a *self-determining power* in their supposed *free wills* while they deny it to the Most High God, and insist upon it that His choice of some men to salvation rather than others, is from either a *foresight* or *aftersight* of good dispositions and "good doings" in them more than others, so making that to be **the cause** of His choice which He declares plainly is the *effect* of it, and representing that God is influenced in His work by motives **without** Himself, at the same time that they hold a power to determine all *their own* actions **within** themselves! Can any imagination ever be entertained more absurd or more contrary to Holy Writ and sound reasoning than these are? *"I thank Thee, O Father, Lord of heaven and earth, because Thou hast hid these things from the wise and prudent, and hast revealed them unto babes. Even so, Father: for so it seemed good in Thy sight. **All things** are delivered unto Me of My Father: and no man knoweth the Son, but the Father; neither knoweth any man the Father, save the Son, and he to whomsoever the Son will **reveal** Him"* (Matthew 11:25-27); *"For whom He did foreknow, He also did predestinate to be conformed to the image of His Son, that He might be the Firstborn among* *many brethren. Moreover whom He did predestinate, them He also called: and whom He called, them He also justified: and whom He justified, them He also glorified"* (Romans 8: 29,30); *"According as He hath chosen us in Him before the foundation of the world, that we should be* **holy and without blame before Him** *in love: having predestinated us unto the adoption of children by Jesus Christ to Himself, according to the* **good pleasure of His will"** (Ephesians 1: 4,5); *"Elect according to the foreknowledge of God the Father, through* **sanctification of the Spirit***, unto obedience and sprinkling of the blood of Jesus Christ"* (I John 4:19).

The people we are now speaking of commonly deny the doctrine of **man's universal depravity,** but if to claim a sovereignty of **their own will,** they deny it to God, does not prove them to be rebels against heaven, I know not what can do it.

Nebuchadnezzar made trial how it would do to ascribe all his achievements to himself, but after he had grazed among the beasts of the field till seven times had passed over him, he declares that, *"All the inhabitants of the earth are reputed as* **nothing** (before the Most High) *and He doth according to* **HIS WILL** *in the army of heaven, and* **among the inhabitants of the earth***: and none can stay*

His hand, or say unto Him, What doest Thou?" (Daniel 4:35). Thus it happens that *"the king's heart is in the hand of the Lord, as the rivers of water:* **He turned it whithersoever He will"** (Proverb 21:1), and if so of kings, or absolute monarchs, how much more of lesser men than kings? That is, while the king acts *voluntarily* as he designs yet only as **God designed** to have them to do. From hence it appears evident that there is no inconsistency in holding **God's decrees to be immutable,** yet that **men act as voluntarily** *as if* it were not so. And the great reasoners on the other side cannot avoid this consequence, if they would once own that the **will** of man is **always determined** in its choice *by motive* or by what they at present prefer and think to be best, for that person must be stupid indeed who cannot see that *"He in whom we live, move, and have our being,"* can at any time set things in such a view before our minds as to make us think it best to choose one way of acting rather than another, which proves the will of man is not "free." Do not men often do the same to other men as well? Though Balaam was so madly set after the *"wages of unrighteousness"* that he would not be turned even by the reproof of a

dumb ass, yet when the Lord opened his eyes to see the angel with a drawn sword before him, he at once **choose** to fall to the earth or to turn back rather than run upon it! (Numbers 22:31). In order therefore to keep up their conceit and delusion that **eternally fixed decrees** interfere with men's liberty, some of their greatest "doctors" have:

Fourth. Tried to shelter themselves in such a miserable refuge as to pretend that they have *a power in **their wills** to act with motive or against motive just as their will pleases.* But I suppose it is as great a piece of nonsense in itself to hold that a rational soul can act voluntarily in any case without or against *motive*, as it would be to say there can be a rational action without any influence of reason in it! Thus *"professing themselves to be wise, they became fools,"* for as Mr. John Locke truly observes, even delirious persons are influenced by reason only they reason from wrong premises. As when such a man imagines that he is all made of glass; he is moved to act with the caution that would be necessary if the case were so. And the like may be said of other imaginations. And persons must be idiots and not reason at all, or else reason and motive will **always influence their choice and conduct. Evil imaginations and thoughts** *always* **move men to act wickedly**, *"But unto Cain and his offering He had not respect. And Cain was very*

wroth, and his countenance fell" and *"Cain talked with Abel his brother: and it came to pass when they were in the field, Cain rose up against Abel his brother, and slew him"* (Genesis 4: 5,8). But when any are brought to know the truth it makes them free, free from sin's dominion, so as to become *"servants of* **righteousness***"* (John 8:31, & Romans 6:18). The main objections I ever heard against Sovereign Election and certain salvation, by free grace alone, appear to me to spring from this root, viz., Man, who was flattered with the notion of "being as gods" still conceits that he has a "power of will in himself" to do as he pleases, let that pleasure be to comply with or to disappoint **God's** *designs;* and therefore, if they are not disposed at present to engage in His service, that He must wait their leisure, and be ready, whenever *they set about the work* in good earnest, to grant them the assistance of His grace and, if they improve it well unto the end, then to
receive them to His glory. But for my part, I have no more notion of worshiping a deity that can possibly be mistaken or disappointed in any one event, than I have of worshiping Baal, who could not defend either his altar or grove when his votaries were asleep (Judges 6:31).

Those who are determined to believe nothing but what they can *comprehend,* are determined to be idolaters, for 'tis certain that anything that can be comprehended by a finite mind cannot be the Infinite Jehovah whose wisdom, knowledge and judgments are *"unsearchable and His ways past finding out; of whom, through whom and to whom **are all things**; to whom be glory forever, amen"* (Romans 11: 33-36). Thus to believe, adore, and obey is not, as many would have it, a sacrificing of *reason* to *tradition* and blind devotion, but the contrary. As, for instance, should any man conceit that he could not know whether or not there was light in the sun or warmth in the fire without looking through the one and running into the other, and should try the experiment till he became blind or burnt, he could not from thence convince me that I had lost both my sight and feeling because I still professed to enjoy great comfort in the cautious improvement of those blessings. Now the perfections of God are compared both to the sun and fire, to teach us the importance of receiving His grace as "free gifts", of acting towards Him uprightly, and serving of Him with *"reference and Godly fear"* (Psalm 84:11; & Hebrews 12: 28,29).

Some serious persons are afraid to **give in to the doctrine of immutable decrees lest they should *make God the author of sin*,** but Mr Norton, one of the fathers of this country [Signer of the Declaration of Independence- Ed], justly replied to this objection that "sin is a defect, and God is the author of all efficiency but not of any defect at all." An illegitimate child is the creature of God, but its illegitimacy is wholly from its parents (see Genesis 49:10 with 38: 15-29, with Matthew 1:3). It was *their* lusts that caused the *defect* or want of its being lawfully (before men) begotten. Yet the child is God's creature, and if He pleases He makes it a subject of His grace, as with any other child. The heat of the sun that attacks the secret virtues of the earth is not the *cause* of the stink of the dunghill. And though reasoners try to persuade people that to hold to absolute predestination, that every event to be **certain** in the Divine counsel takes away the guilt of evil actions, and the virtue of good ones; yet the Word of Truth abundantly shows the contrary. It shows that Joseph's brethren were as verily guilty in their actions against him as if they could have frustrated God's design, and yet that He **over-ruled** their wrath and cruelty towards their brother, for His own praise, (Psalm 56:10) and to make Joseph much more of a public and extensive blessing than they could have made him in Canaan, if they had tried their uttermost for it. At the same time the sacred story clearly shows that they acted quite voluntarily, both in their wretched abuses to their brother, and in humbly prostrating themselves before him afterward, they acted by motives; when they first saw Joseph coming to them, they felt so that they thought they would slay the dreamer. But upon another view murder appeared so shocking that they thought it best to gratify themselves another way, which moved them to choose that way – so they sold him instead, fulfilling the very dreams that were told to them and for which cause they hated him. On the other hand, when Joseph was tempted by his wicked mistress, though men were absent, yet God to whom he was under infinite obligation, was present in his thoughts, and that proved a sufficient motive to make him choose any suffering rather than to sin against such a glorious Being.

The inquiry and pursuit of all men is after *good*, and the believer finds it only in God, who is *good* and is always doing *good*, and this causes his soul to be in earnest to *"learn His statutes"* (Psalm 4: 6,7 and 119: 68). Others do not like to retain the true God in their knowledge; neither His nature nor His government appears good to their carnal minds. Therefore they *"worship and serve the creature more than the Creator"* (Romans 1:25), setting up gain, honor, or pleasure as their chief good. Yet to appear nakedly irreligious is too shocking to multitudes, who at the same time are far from desiring to set the Lord always before them, so as to be influenced by Him in all their conduct. Therefore they choose their *idol shepherds* that will prophesy *smooth things* to them rather than faithful watchmen who represent the true character of the *"Holy One of Israel before them"* (Isaiah 30: 8-11; Zechariah 11:17).

A darling topic with the carnal reasoners of our world is this: they say that either men are *able to obey and serve God,* or else, if they *cannot do it,* until God is pleased to convert them, they are not to blame for neglecting of it; that God will never command a man to do what he cannot do. To them, this is contrary to *their* natural reason. But the truth is, the natural man **cannot serve God because he does love and serve an idol.** And the soul before it is slain by the law, **cannot be married to Christ** because it is **wedded** to its own doings (Matthew 6:24; Romans 7). Yet this inability is so far from being any just excuse that the more unable they are to love God or to believe in Christ the greater is their *"condemnation"* (John 3: 16,19).

It is a most wicked device in the writer of the paper now in hand, to use the word *inevitable* concerning **reprobates** and *irresistible,* concerning the **elec**t in such a manner as to exclude the idea of their own wicked choice; whereas the vessels of wrath say, *"We **will walk after our own devices,** and we will every one do the imagination of **his evil heart**"* (Jeremiah 18:12) and of such the Lord said, *"For every one that doeth evil hateth the light, neither cometh to the light, lest his deeds should be reproved"* (John 3:20). The vessels of mercy pursue the same ways till God **works in them** *"to will and to do of His good pleasure," "working **in them** that which is well pleasing in His sight, through Jesus Christ, to whom be glory for ever and ever"* (Philippians 2:13, Hebrews 13:21). Therefore though the final event **is as certain** to the one as the other, yet in the manner of its accomplishments is vastly different. The vessels of wrath, *"after their hard and impenitent heart, treasure up wrath **to themselves,** while God endureth with much longsuffering with them,"* but He *"makes known"* the riches of His glory in effectually *"calling the vessels of mercy which He had **afore prepared unto glory"*** (Romans 2:5 and 9:22-24). And renewed souls are so far from assuming to themselves a **free will power** to be God's *counselors* or venturing to act upon those *"secret things which belong to God"* (Deuteronomy 29:29), that where He has told them of His designs concerning any future event they have **not made** the *design* of the great Ruler, but **the laws He has given to His subjects the rule of their conduct**; and the great difference between *subjects* and *rebels* is discovered by this. As, for instance, God let David know that He designed to remove Saul and make David king in his stead. Yet David refused to smite Saul when he had opportunity but left it with God to remove him in His own way (I Samuel 24:12,13). Whereas when the Jews heard Caiphas' prophecy concerning the death of Jesus, *"from that day forth, they took counsel together for to put Him to death"* (John 11:49-53). That is quite a difference between the two! And God's accomplishing His **infallible decrees** in that great event, while the Jews were inexcusably guilty – *"ye by wicked hands has seized and slain"* – in their actions about it, are strongly asserted by the inspired apostle. *"Him, being delivered by the* ***determinate counsel and foreknowledge of God, YE have taken, and by WICKED HANDS have crucified and slain"*** (Acts 2:23).

They acted most wickedly in conspiring against the Savior who was perfectly holy and harmless and constantly went about doing good. Yet God's purpose and promises were thereby **exactly accomplished** in bestowing infinite and eternal mercies upon guilty and miserable men. Pharaoh used great subtlety and cruelty in order to keep Israel in bondage and set up **his will** at the highest rate against releasing of them. Yet God in His Providence caused things to appear so to him and his subjects that they **voluntarily furnished Israel with silver and gold,** and *"Egypt was glad when they departed"* (Psalm 105: 37,38), *"and that on the selfsame day"* God told Abraham of above four-hundred years before (Exodus 12:41) !

These and many other instances of men's **voluntary actions,** the Lord declared with a **perfect exactness before they came to pass,** because He **knew** that with a **brazen obstinacy and willful treachery** they would rather give this glory to their **idol** than to Him (Isaiah 48: 3-8).

But the firm faith of the saints in every age in the **certain accomplishment of God's promises** has made them the more watchful and active in the rational choice that He furnished them with for attaining the desired end. Jacob wrestled and prevailed with God, yet that did not make him neglect, but to wisely improve the best that he had in his power to calm his angry brother, and it had the desired effect. Paul believed God that the lives of all those who were with him in the ship should be saved (Acts 27:24), yet when the men who were skilled in managing the ship were about to leave it, he said to the centurion and to the soldiers, "*Except these abide in the ship ye **cannot** be saved*" (Acts 27:25-31). Here was a **certainty of an event,** and yet it is **expressed conditionally,** while **both were true!** It was true that all should be saved, and they were; and it was also true that the mariners must be instrumental of it.

Thus, my dear friend, I have endeavored in as plain and brief a manner as I could, in the little time I had for it, opened and vindicated the great Scriptural **doctrine of GOD'S SOVEREIGN DECREES** against a malicious attempt which has been made to vilify the same. It may well seem surprising to those who are acquainted with the *"Seventeenth Article of the Church of England,"* to hear that a minister who has solemnly engaged to maintain the truth therein expressed, should have a great hand in spreading this blasphemous paper which is diametrically contrary thereto, as has evidently been the case. But I leave him and all others in the hand of a righteous and gracious God, and rest,

Yours, *etc.,* Isaac Backus, 1773, Boston.

THE GREAT FALLING AWAY:
The Last Days In Fulfilment
Isaac Backus, 1773

[The first Old School Baptist Historian in America, Isaac Backus was called out of the Congregational Puritans during the Great Awakening. He compiled *"A History of New England with Particular Reference to The Baptists* in 1777, which made him the first Baptist to write a history on that Christian people. In his life-time, he saw the wonderful modification of the world's political systems and upheaval of the then social order, and the rise of, first, the Confederate government under the Articles of Confederation, its failure, and the planting of the Federal Union under the United States Constitution. Being a minister of the Gospel, he viewed these world events through the instrument of Divine Prophecy as he then understood those events.

We share this, his views, [without endorsement of any millennial views of our own] to the interested reader. THE PUBLISHER.]

Observation On The Foregoing History

How clearly has the word of God been fulfilled! For He says, *"That day shall not come except there come a falling away first, and that **man of sin** be revealed, the son of perdition: who opposeth and exalteth himself above all that is called God, or that is worshipped; so that he, as God, sitteth in the temple of God, shewing himself that he is God. And now ye know what withholdeth, that he might be revealed in his time. For the mystery of iniquity doth already* *work; only he who now letteth [hindereth] will let [hinder] until he be taken out of the way: and then shall that Wicked be revealed, whom the Lord shall consume with the spirit of His mouth, and shall destroy with the brightness of His coming: even him, whose coming is after the working of Satan, with all power, and signs, and lying wonders, and with all deceivableness of unrighteousness in them that perish; because they receive not the love of the truth that they might be saved. And for this cause God shall send them strong delusion that the should believe a lie; that they all might be damned who believe not the truth, but had pleasure in unrighteousness. But we are bound to give thanks always to God for you, brethren, beloved of the Lord, because God hath from the beginning chosen you to salvation, through sanctification of the Spirit, and belief of the truth: whereunto He called you by our Gospel, to obtaining of the glory of our Lord Jesus Christ"* (II Thess. 2:3-14).

Here all men are described as in **two parties.** So our Lord says, *"Every one that doeth evil hateth the light, neither cometh to the light, lest his deeds should be reproved. But he that doeth truth cometh to the light, that his deeds may be made manifest that they* (his deeds) *are **wrought in God"*** (John 3:20,21). It is impossible for God to violate His promise, or His oath, or to entice any into sin (Heb. 6:13-18; James 1:13-14). But all men are guilty of these evils, more or less, who are not born again. And when Constantine removed the seat of his empire from Rome, and then divided it at his death, the way was made for the bishop of Rome to exalt himself above God in his (Constantine's) church, and above all the kings of Europe, who gave their power unto him. And forbidding to marry, and commanding to abstain from meats, was held in that "church" for many centuries before Luther's reformation (1 Tim. 4:1-3).

Yet an external succession of baptisms, and of ministerial power, through all those abominations, is **now held fast** in our land, as we have before proved (in his History- Editor) Yea, and the doctrines of original sin, particular election, efficacious grace in conversion, justification wholly by the faith of Christ in the perfect righteousness of Christ, and the final perseverance of His saints, are being now denied by multitudes in Europe and America. And are they not left to a **strong delusion to believe a lie?** For all the holy priesthood that God has under heaven are, *"**elect** according to the foreknowledge of God the Father, through sanctification of the Spirit, unto obedience, and sprinkling of the blood **of Jesus Christ**"* (I Peter 1:2; 2:5,9). Yet ministers and parents still imagine, that they **can make children** holy members of the church before they can believe for themselves, and holy ministers by an external succession of ordinations. And a minister before named [Joseph Huntington, 1783- Editor, History, page 315] says, "When you re-baptize those in adult years, which we have baptized in their infancy, you and they jointly renounce that Father, Son, and Holy Ghost, whom we adore and worship as the only living and true God, and on whom we depend for all our salvation. [This same minister embraced universal salvation, and died in 1795] – Editor]. So some Jewish teachers had said, *"Except ye be circumcised, after the manner of Moses, ye cannot be saved"* (Acts 15:1). But the Holy Ghost, in the church at

Jerusalem, said, "*Why tempt ye God, to put a yoke upon the neck of the disciples, which neither our fathers nor we were able to bear?*" (Acts 15:1,10). The Sinai covenant yoked believers and unbelievers together. And another minister says, "Some who are not inwardly sanctified, are yet so far in covenant, that they are rightful members of the visible church, as all but the Anabaptists must grant." And again he says, "It is certain that the rule of admission is such,[In Protestant churches] that some, yea, many unsanctified persons may be, and are regularly admitted to church membership. All the *congregations* of Israel were admitted as members of the visible church by God Himself at Mount Sinai; yet who will say that one in ten of them were **saints in heart**? The children of believers are *reputed* saints, and as such, have a right of admission; yet we are not sure that the greater part of them are inwardly sanctified from the womb, or even afterwards." [Hemmenway on the Church, pp.29,49]. Yea, we are so far from seeing any evidence of inward sanctification in most of the children of professors, that they generally evidence the contrary in their lives as much as other men. And when the church of Israel were entering upon the promise land, Moses said, "*The Lord hath not given you an heart to perceive, and eyes to see, and ears to hear unto this day*" (Deuteronomy 29:4). So far was he from giving them any idea that all their national church were inwardly sanctified.

But a little before the Babylonian captivity, it was said, "*Behold, the days come, saith the Lord, that I will make a **new covenant** with the house of Israel, and with the house of Judah; **not according** to the* *covenant that I made with their fathers in the day that I took them by the hand, to bring them out of the land of Egypt (which My covenant they brake, although I was an husband unto them, saith the Lord;) but this shall be the covenant that I will make with the house of Israel, After those days, saith the Lord, I will put My law in their inward parts, and write it in their hearts, and will be their God, and they shall be My people: and they shall not teach no more every man his neighbor, and every man his brother, saying, Know the Lord: for they shall all know Me, from the least of them unto the greatest of them, saith the Lord; for I will forgive their iniquity, and I will remember their sin no more"* (Jeremiah 31: 31-34). And this is the covenant upon which the true Gospel Church is built. (Hebrews 8:8-12). And it is as distinct from the covenant of circumcision with the nation of Israel, as Sarah was from Hagar, or Zion from Sinai; yea, as distinct as Jerusalem which is above, and is free, being the mother of all the children of God, is from Jerusalem below, which is in bondage with her children. (Galatians 4:22-26). And language cannot make a clearer distinction, than is here made, between the nation covenant with Israel, and the covenant of grace with the true church of Christ.

When the Jews returned from Babylon, and began to build the temple, their enemies sent false accusations against them to the court of Persia, and procured an order from thence to force them to cease from that work. But after another king came to the throne, two prophets were raised up, to reprove the Jews for their negligence, and to encourage them to finish the house of God. (Ezra 4:11-24, 5:1,2). And because the old men wept to see how much inferior this house was, to the glorious temple which was built by Solomon, one prophet said to them, *"I am with you, saith the Lord of hosts; according to the word that I covenanted with you when ye came out of Egypt, so My Spirit remaineth among you; fear ye not. For this saith the Lord of host, Yet once, it is a little while, and I will shake the heavens and the earth, and the sea, and the dry land; and I will shake all nations, and the Desire of all Nations shall come, and I will fill this house with glory, saith the Lord of Hosts.* (Hag. 2:4-7).* And after the Son of God came and taught in that house, as no man ever did before, and then offered Himself a sacrifice to God for the sins of His elect people, and arose and ascended to Heaven, and gave the Holy Ghost from thence, to enable His ministers to preach the Gospel to Jews and Gentiles, an inspired apostle said, *"Yet once more, signifieth the removing of those things that are shaken, as of things that are made, that those things which cannot be shaken may remain. Wherefore, we receiving a kingdom which cannot be moved, let us have grace, whereby we may serve God acceptably, with reverence and godly fear; for our God is a consuming fire"* (Heb. 12: 27-29).

The other prophet had a lamp stand all of gold, set before him, with mediums to convey oil into it for light; and upon his inquiry what was meant thereby, the answer was, *"This is the word of the Lord unto Zerubbabel, saying, Not by might, nor by power, but by My Spirit, saith the Lord of hosts. Who art thou, O great mountain? Before Zerubbabel thou shalt become a plain, and he shall bring forth the Headstone thereof, with shoutings, crying,* **Grace, grace** *unto it !"* (Zech. 4:107). And when they obeyed this call of

God, their enemies wrote again to the court of Persia against them, but a decree in their favor was procured thereby, and all was plain before them. (Ezra 5:7-17; 6: 1-16). The golden lamp stand represented the church of God, and the two olive trees were His precepts and promises, whereby He poured the oil of His grace into His church, to hold up light to the world, who hated it because it tormented their consciences. Before the coming of Christ there was but one lamp stand, with two olive trees to pour oil into it; but when Christ came He broke down the middle wall of partition between Jews and Gentiles, and built His church upon the foundation of the apostles and prophets, for an habitation of God through the Spirit (Ephesians 2: 14-22).

And when antichrist arose, God said, *"I will give power unto My two witnesses, and they shall prophecy a thousand two hundred and threescore days, clothed in sackcloth."* These are the two olive trees, and the two lamp stands standing before the God of the earth. And it is to be observed, that the church is in the wilderness, and the beast continues all the time that these witnesses prophecy in sackcloth. (Rev. 11:3,4; 12:6; and 13:5). The two Testaments, believed, loved and obeyed by the children of God, appear to be the two witnesses.

And a being anointed by the Spirit of Christ, is essential to the name Christian. For the disciples were not called by that name, until after the Gentiles were received into the church without circumcision (Acts 11:26). And it is said, *"If ye be reproached for the name of Christ, happy are ye; for the **Spirit** of glory, and of God resteth upon you; on their part He is* *evil spoken of, but on your part He is glorified. But let none of you suffer as a murderer, or as a thief, or as an evil doer, or as a busy body in other men's matters. Yet if any man suffer as a* **Christian***, let him not be ashamed; but let him glorified God on this behalf* (I Peter 4:14-16). *"Ye are not in the flesh, but in the* **Spirit***, if so be the Spirit of God dwell in you. Now if any man have not the* **Spirit** *of Christ, he is none of His"* (Romans 8:9). Again, it is said, *"Hereby we know that He abideth in us, by the* **Spirit** *which He hath given us"* (I John 3:24). And Jesus said, *"If a man love Me, he will keep My words, and My Father will love him, and we will come unto him, and make our abode with him"* (John 14:23). *"Whosoever transgresseth, and abideth not in the doctrine of Christ, hath not God; he that abideth in the doctrine of Christ, he hath both the Father and the Son. If there come any unto you, and bringeth not this doctrine, receive him not into your house, neither bid him God-speed; for he that biddeth him God-speed is partaker of his evil deeds"* (II John 1:9).

And how clearly do these things shew, that no person can be a Christian without a change of heart by the Spirit of Christ! Yea, and that receiving and supporting true ministers, and refusing to receive false teachers, is ever a matter between God and individuals, as much as faith in Christ is for eternal salvation! And no man can have any more right to support religious teachers by the sword, than they have power to pull down the Son of God from His throne in heaven. For He says, *"All they that take the sword, shall perish with the sword"* (Matt. 26:52). *"My kingdom is not of this world; if My kingdom were of this world, then would My servants fight, that I should not be delivered to the Jews; but now is My kingdom not from hence"* (John 18:36). How then will any men dare to support religious ministers by the sword of the magistrates? For his power is to punish none but those who work ill to their neighbors; and it is a matter of conscience with true Christians to be subject to such rulers, who are not a terror to good works, but to the evil. (Romans 8:1-10. But the royal prophet says of wicked rulers, *"They break in pieces Thy people, O Lord, and afflict Thine heritage. They slay the widow and stranger, and murder the fatherless. Yet they say, The Lord shall not see, neither shall the God of Jacob regard it"* (Psalm 94:5-7,20). *Shall the throne of iniquity have fellowship with Thee, which frameth mischief by a law?. . . . The Lord at thy right hand shall strike through kings in the day of His wrath. He shall judge among the heathen, He shall fill the places with dead bodies, He shall wound the heads over many countries"* (Psalm 110:5,6). And how awfully is He now doing it! (Rev. 19:11-21).

And is it not evident that the late increase of Baptist churches has been caused by the influence of the Spirit of God? [the "Great Awakening" phenomenon, 1720-1770 - Editor] For before He poured out His Spirit in the county of Hampshire (New Hampshire), in and after 1734, there were but six Baptist churches **in all of New England**, except Rhode Island government, wherein are now **two hundred and eighty-five churches**. And in these four States, where "established" ministers have been supported by law, all the power of such ministers and rulers has been against the Baptist churches; and they have found so much difficulty in supporting their own ministers, and in guarding against oppression from others, that some societies have obtained incorporations by the laws *of men!* But our Associations have published testimonies against all such incorporations, as they implicitly deny that the laws and Spirit of Christ are sufficient to govern His church, and to support His ministers. And while they act all the affairs of their Associations openly, before all men who have a mind to hear them, and then publish their conclusions to the world, how can they hope for any earthly advantage thereby? If heavenly influence has not increased their churches, what cause can be assigned therefore?

All true believers in Christ are *"born again, not of blood, nor of the will of the flesh, nor of the will of man, but of God"* (John 1:12-13). Natural descent, the power of our own wills, and of the wills of other men, are all excluded from this affair. And where the opposite principles have crept into Baptist churches, their welfare has been obstructed thereby, and many such churches have been dissolved. Yet the word and Spirit of God have reformed old churches, and raised many new ones in all parts of America.

There was one Baptist church in all of Virginia, and a few in the Carolinas seventy years ago; but they were dark and feeble societies until some spiritual preachers were sent among them, in and after 1753. The elders, Benjamin Miller, Isaac Stelle, Peter Peterson Vanhorn, and John Gano, went from New Jersey and Pennsylvania, and labored in those parts to good purpose. Later Elder Shubael Stearns, Daniel Marshall, and others, went from Connecticut, and spent their lives in those parts, as was before observed; and how great has been the increase of the Baptist churches in those Southern States! And though vast pains have been taken, by men who have supported their worship by force, to make the people believe that the Baptists were enemies to good government, yet how are they now confounded in those attempts! For it now appears that government and liberty are united in their plan of conduct, which tends to bring all wars to an end. And in a prophecy concerning that glorious event, it is said, *"All people will walk every one in the name of his god, and we will walk in the name of the Lord our God forever and ever"* (Micah 4:5). All men who love any creature above the Creator are idolaters.

But our Lord says, *"If ye keep **My** commandments, ye shall abide in My love; even as I have kept My Father's commandment, and abide in His love. . . . If ye were of the world, the world would love his own; but because ye are not of the world, but I have chosen you out of the world, therefore the world hateth you"* (John 15:19). How then will any men dare to confound the church and the world together in religious affairs? For as long as natural birth could bring the children of Israel into the church, and into the priesthood, God said to them, *"The man that committeth adultery with another man's wife, even he that committeth adultery with his neighbor's wife, the adulterer and the adulteress shall surely be put to death"* (Lev. 20:10). And He now says to all the world, *"Ye adulterers and adulteresses, know ye not that the friendship of the world is enmity with God? Whosoever therefore will be a friend of the world, is the enemy of God. . . . . There is one Lawgiver, who is able to save, and to destroy; who art thou that judgest another?"* (James 4:4,12). Yet men in general have assumed the power of lawgivers and judges for the church of Christ, and of bringing children into it before they could believe for themselves; and they have invented a multitude of other names and denominations of men, besides the righteous and the wicked, the church and the world. Though the word of revelation says, *"Whosoever is born of God, doth not commit sin; for His seed remaineth in him; and he cannot sin, because he is born of God. In this the children of God are manifest, and the children of the devil: whosoever doeth not righteousness, is not of God, neither he that loveth not his brother. For this is the message that ye have heard from the beginning, that we should love one another. Not as Cain, who was of that wicked one, and slew his brother: and wherefore slew he him? Because his own works were evil, and his brother's righteous"* (I John 3:9-12). *"Woe unto them; for they have gone in the way of Cain, and ran greedily after the error of Balaam for reward,* [a hired minister], *and perished in the gainsaying of Core* [Who said all of God's people could prophesy] *"* (Jude 11). Because the worship of Abel, by faith in the shed blood of Christ, was accepted of God, and the worship of Cain without such faith was not accepted, he was filled with envy against his brother. But the Lord said unto Cain, *"If thou doest well, shalt thou be accepted? And if thou doest not well, sin lieth at the door. And unto thee shall be his desire, and thou shalt rule over him"* (Genesis 4:4-7). True believers have ever been the best subjects of civil government; but men have discovered enmity against them in every age, because of the light of holiness which God hath caused to shine in their lives, to expose the hypocrisy and wickedness of others. **But every man is guilty of**

adultery, who hath not been made dead to the works of the law, in order to be married to Jesus Christ" (Romans 7:1-6). For every true Christian hath been presented as a chaste virgin to Him" (II Cor. 11:2)

But after God had consecrated Moses as the lawgiver to His church in the wilderness, and Aaron and his lawful posterity to be the only priests therein, to offer sacrifices for iniquity, until Jesus came and offered Himself without spot to God for sinners, Korah gathered a large company against them, saying, *"Ye take too much upon you, seeing all the congregation are holy every one of them, and the Lord is among them: wherefore then lift you up yourselves above the congregation of the Lord?* But for this they perished most terribly. (Numbers 16:1-3,32-33). This gives a plain view of the "way of Cain, the error of Balaam, and the gainsaying of Core," which evils many today have charged upon believers, because they have held tenaciously to salvation by faith in the perfect righteousness of Christ, and to have His church governed by His laws, which admit *none into it without a credible profession of the new birth.* Thus men have called evil good, and good evil; have put darkness for light, and light for darkness, bitter for sweet, and sweet for bitter throughout the ages. (Isa. 5:20).

But an inspired apostle says, *"We have received not the spirit of the world, but the Spirit which is of God, that we might know the things that are freely given us of God. Which things also we speak, not in the words which man's wisdom teacheth, but which the Holy Ghost teacheth; comparing spiritual things with spiritual"* (I Cor. 2:12,13). Let us now attend to this rule. For God says, *"Thy Maker is thine husband* (the Lord of host is His name)*; and thy Redeemer, the Holy One of Israel, the God of the whole earth shall He be called. ....And all thy children shall be taught of the Lord, and great shall be the peace of thy children"* (Isa. 54:5,13). And Jesus says, *"No man can come to Me, except the Father which hath sent Me, draw him; and I will raise him up at the last day. It is written in the prophets, And they shall be all taught of God. Every man therefore that hath heard, and hath learned of the Father, cometh unto Me"* (John 6:44-45). The *children* of the church of Christ, are *men*, who have been taught of God, (not by men) and have learned of the Father (and not of men), so as to come to the Son. So Paul says, *"Jerusalem which is above is free, which is the mother of us all"* (Galatians 4:26). And John says, *"I saw the holy city, Jerusalem, coming down from God out of heaven, prepared as a bride adorned for her Husband"* (Rev. 21:2). And Jesus says, *"Give not that which is holy unto the dogs, neither cast ye your pearls before swine, lest they trample them under their feet, and turn again and rend you. ....The kingdom of heaven is like unto a merchantman, seeking goodly pearls; who when he had found one pearl of great price, he went and sold all that he had, and bought it"* (Matt. 7:6; 13: 45-46). *"So likewise, whosoever he be of you, that forsaketh not all that he hath, he cannot be My disciple"* (Luke 14:33). *"Except a man be born again, he cannot see the kingdom of God"* (John 3:3). *"Every several gate was of one -pearl. Blessed are they that do His commandments, that they may have right to the tree of life, and may enter in through the gates into the city. For without are dogs, and sorcerers, and*

-130-

whoremongers, and adulterers, and whosoever loveth and maketh a lie. I, Jesus. Have sent Mine angel to testify unto you these things in the churches. I am the root and the offspring of David, and the bright and morning star. And the Spirit and the Bride say, Come; and let him that heareth, say Come; and let him that is athirst, come; and whosoever will, let him take the water of life freely" (Rev. 21:21; 22: 14-17). How clearly do these things show, that the government of the church of Christ is as distinct from all worldly governments, as heaven is from earth! Yea, and that no one has any **true right in His church, until he comes to Christ by faith which worketh by** *love* **that is as free as water!** For God says, *"In the last days it shall come to pass, that the mountain of the house of the Lord shall be established in the top of the mountains, and it shall be exalted above the hills, and people shall* ***flow*** *into it. And many nations shall come and say, Come and let us go up to the mountain of the Lord, and to the house of the God of Jacob, and* **He** *will teach us His ways, and we will walk in His paths; for the law shall go forth of Zion, and the word of the Lord from Jerusalem. And He shall judge among many people, and rebuke strong nations afar off, and they shall beat their swords into ploughshares, and their spears into pruning-hooks; nations shall not lift up sword against nation, neither shall they learn war any more"* (Micah 4:1-3). Now all men may know, that this prophecy has never yet been fulfilled; but it will as surely be accomplished, as any prophecy ever was in this world. How earnest then should all be to hear and obey the revealed will of God!

And no man can obey Him without denying himself, and taking up his cross, and following the example of Christ. And the apostle says to the ministers of Christ, *"I have not shunned to declare unto you the counsel of God. Take heed therefore unto yourselves, and to all the flock, over the which the Holy Ghost hath made you overseers, to feed the church of God, which He hath purchased with His own blood. For I know this, that after my departing shall grievous wolves enter in among you, not sparing the flock. Also of yourselves shall men arise, speaking perverse things, to draw away disciples after them. Therefore watch, and remember that by the space of three years, I cease not to warn every one night and day with tears. And now, brethren, I command you to God, and to the word of His grace, which is able to build you up, and to give you an inheritance among all them which are sanctified. I have coveted no man's silver, or gold, or apparel. Yea, you yourselves know that these hands have ministered unto my necessities, and to them that were with me. I have shewed you all things, how that so laboring ye ought to support the weak; and to remember the words of the Lord Jesus, how He said, 'It is more blessed to give than to receive"* (Acts 20:27-35). And how has this prophecy been fulfilled in every age since it was published! And how **few believe** that God, and the word of His grace, is **able to build up His church,** and to guard against grievous wolves, and against perverse schismatics, without the laws of men enforced by the sword! Yea, how much has the sword promoted both of these evils! And how little do we believe, that it is more blessed to give than to receive! It is blessed to receive, when we receive in a right manner; but all things below perish in the using, while all that is given for the benefit of the bodies or souls of others, is laying up treasure in heaven, which will turn to praise, honor and glory at the appearing of Jesus Christ. And though Paul had written to the church of Corinth, upon their duty to support the preachers of the Gospel, yet as deceitful teachers had tried to destroy his character, pretending that he acted from selfish motives, he refused to receive any support from them himself, until he could come and have those accusations tried before that church, in the mouth of two or three witnesses, according to the law of Christ. But as his refusal to receive any thing of them, as he did of other churches, might seem to be a dishonor to the church of Corinth, he said, *"Forgive me this wrong"* (II Cor. 11:12; 12:13; 13:1-4). This shows that **a particular church of Christ is the highest judicature that He has established upon earth, to carry His laws into execution in His name. And the people also are to act towards their ministers as they can answer it to God in the last day.** For he says, *"The laborer is worthy of his reward"* (I Timothy 5:18). *"Let him that is taught in the word, communicate unto him that teacheth in all good things. Be not deceived: God is not mocked; for whatsoever a man soweth, that shall he also reap. For he that soweth to the flesh, shall reap of the flesh corruption; but he that soweth to the Spirit, shall of the Spirit reap life everlasting. And let us not be weary in well doing; for in due season we shall reap, if we faint not"* (Galatians 6:6-9). Thus ministers and people alike are required to act towards each other, as they can answer the same to God, who only can bless or curse them in time and/or eternity. And Christ says to His ministers, *"He that heareth **you**, heareth **Me**; and he that **despiseth you, despiseth Me;** and he* that despiseth Me, **despiseth Him that sent Me**" (Luke 10:16). And how solemn are these considerations! Yea, and how safe are all true believers in Christ!

For He says, "*Upon this Rock I will build **My church;** and the gates of hell shall not prevail against it*" (Matt. 16:18). And though many have made strange work of this saying, and others have paid no regard to it, yet many ancient passages may serve to explain its vast importance. For it is said of God's people of old, "*When He slew them, then they sought Him; and they returned and inquired early after God. And they remembered that God was their Rock, and the high God their Redeemer. Nevertheless they did flatter Him with their mouth, and they **lied** unto Him with their tongues; for their **heart** was not right with Him, neither were they steadfast in His covenant*" (Psalm 78: 34-37). "*Wherefore hear the word of the Lord, ye scornful men that rule this people which are in Jerusalem. Because ye have said, 'We have made a covenant with death, and with hell are we at agreement; when the overflowing scourge shall pass through, it shall not come unto us; for we have made **lies** our refuge, and under falsehood have we hid ourselves;' therefore thus saith the Lord God, "Behold, I lay in Zion for a foundation, a stone, a tried stone, a precious corner-stone, a sure foundation; he that believeth shall not make haste. Judgment also will I lay to the line, and righteousness to the plummet, and the hail shall sweep away the refuge of lies, and the waters shall overflow the hiding place; and your covenant with death shall be disannulled, and your agreement with hell shall not stand*" (Isaiah 28:14-18). This prophecy is applied to them who followed after the law of righteousness, but sought it not by faith in Christ, but as it were by the works of the law. *"They had a zeal of God, but not according to knowledge. For they being ignorant of God's righteousness, and going about to establish their own righteousness, have not submitted themselves unto the righteousness of God.`For Christ is the end of the law for righteousness to every one that believeth. And whoever believeth on Him, shall not be ashamed"* (Romans 9:31-33). *"He that believeth on Him shall not be confounded"* (I Peter 2:6). From whence we may learn, that all men who trust in their own doings, instead of the perfect righteousness of Christ, are in covenant with death, and at agreement with hell. And earthly monarchy has generally been the darling of such men! Therefore God says to them, *"Thou wentest to the king with ointment, and didst increase thy perfumes, and didst send thy messengers afar off, and didst debase thyself even unto hell. Thou are wearied in the greatness of thy way, yet sadist thou not, There is no hope; thou hast found the life of thine hand, therefore thou wast not grieved"* (Isaiah 17:9,10). David and his race of kings were *anointed* of the Lord to their office, as eminent types of Christ. And the rage of hypocrites and infidels, against the Lord, and against His *anointed*, was against His *Christ"* (Psalm 2:2; Acts 4:26)). And every child of God has the same *anointing* of His Spirit abiding in him, which effectually teacheth the soul to abide in Christ. (I John 2:27). But the calling any ruler, since the death of Christ, the Lord's anointed, and the setting up any earthly heads to the church, is a practice which came from hell, from the bottomless pit; and this is the beast who causeth God's witnesses to prophesy in mourning, and at length kills them. (Rev. 11:7; 13:1,2,12; and 17:8).

The saints have a gradual victory over him (the beast). For John says, *"I saw as it were a sea of glass, mingled with fire; and them that had gotten the victory over the beast, and over his image, and over his mark, and over the number of his name, stand on the sea of glass, having the harps of God. And they sing the song of Moses, the servant of God, and the song of the Lamb, saying, Great and marvelous are Thy works, Lord God Almighty; just and true are Thy ways, Thou King of saints. Who shall not fear Thee, O Lord, and glorify Thy name? for Thou only art holy; for all nations shall come and worship before Thee, for Thy judgments are made manifest"* (Rev. 15:2-4). The sea of glass, mingled with fire, is the word of God, enforced upon the souls of men by His Holy Spirit. For one apostle says, *"Where the Spirit of the Lord is, there is liberty. But we all with open face, beholding as in a **glass** the glory of the Lord, are changed into the same image, from glory to glory, even as by the Spirit of the Lord"* (II Cor. 3:17,18). And another says, *"Lay apart all filthiness, and superfluity of naughtiness, and receive with meekness the engrafted word, which is able to save your souls. But be ye doers of the word, and not hearers only, deceiving your own selves. For if any be a hearer of the word, and not a doer, he is like unto a man beholding his natural face in a **glass**; for he beholdeth himself, and goeth his way, and straightway forgetteth what manner of man he was. But whoso looketh into the perfect law of liberty, and continueth therein, he being not a forgetful hearer, but a doer of the word, this man shall be blessed **in** his deed"* (James 1:21-25). And when a prophet met with cruel treatment, he said, *"I will not make mention of Him, nor speak any more in His name. But His word was in mine heart as a burning **fire** shut up in my bones, and I was weary with forbearing, and I could not stay."* And God says, *"The prophet that hath a dream, let him tell a dream; and he that hath My word, let him speak My word faithfully; what is the chaff to the wheat? Saith the Lord. Is not My word like as a **fire**? Saith the Lord, and like a hammer that breaketh the rock in pieces?"* (Jeremiah 20:9; 23:28-29). Therefore they who stand upon the sea of glass mingled with fire, are they who hear and obey the revealed will of the Lord. Moses was the lawgiver to the church of Israel, and the Lamb is so to the church of God among all nations. And Moses verily was faithful in all his house as a servant, for a testimony of those things which were to be spoken after; but Christ as a Son over His own house; whose house are we, if we hold fast the confidence, and the rejoicing of the hope firm unto the end. . . . .Now faith is the substance of things hoped for, the evidence of things not seen" (Heb. 3:5,6 and 11:1). And how clearly do these passages prove, that true believers in Christ are the only persons of whom His house or church is composed! For no others can hold fast the confidence, and the rejoicing of hope of salvation in Jesus Christ. The beast appears to be the Church of Rome, over many nations; his image, are all national churches; his mark is the supporting of worship by taxation and compulsion, and the number of his name includes all the schemes of men to hold the church in bondage, so that she might not be governed wholly by the ways of Christ.

This may lead us to consider, what is intended by the killing and resurrection of the two witnesses. If they are the two parts of the Holy Scriptures, believed and obeyed by the children of God, then their death is the triumphing of the ungodly and religious world over them. And the prophecy says, *"When they shall have finished their testimony, the beast that ascendeth out of the bottomless pit shall make war against them, and shall overcome them, and kill them. And their dead bodies shall lie in the street of the great city, which spiritually is called Sodom and Egypt, where also our Lord was crucified. And they of the people, and kindreds, and tongues, and nations, shall see their dead bodies three days and an half, and shall not suffer their dead bodies to be put in graves. And they that dwell upon the earth shall rejoice over them, and make merry, and shall send gifts one to another; because these two prophets tormented them that dwelt on the earth"* (Rev. 11:7-10). Our Lord was crucified by hypocrites and infidels; and He declared those hypocrites to be worse than the old Sodomites" (Matt 11:23,24 and Luke 10:12). And God said in prophecy, *"Sodom thy sister hath not done, she nor her daughters, as thou hast done, thou and thy daughters. Behold, this was the iniquity of Sodom, pride, fullness of bread, and abundance of idleness was in her and in her daughters, neither did she strengthen the hand of the poor and needy. And they were haughty, and committed abomination before Me; therefore I took them away as I saw good. Neither hath Samaria committed half thy sins; but thou hast multiplied thine abominations more than they. . . . .Nevertheless, I will remember My covenant with thee in the days of thy youth, and I will establish unto thee an everlasting covenant. Then thou shalt remember thy ways, and be ashamed, when thou receive thy sisters, thine elder and thy younger; and I will give them unto thee for daughters, but not by thy covenant"* (Ezek. 16: 48-51, 60-61). According to which prophecy, the church of Christ was erected in Jerusalem, and she received the Samaritans, and then the Gentiles into the church as daughters, but not by the covenant of circumcision, which the Jews were in after the Samaritans were separated form them. But this *proverb,* this high *figure* which God delivered to Jerusalem, is now held up as a *literal prophecy,* that all the old Sodomites will finally be saved from hell!(Winchester's Dialogues, pp. 197-200). Though God said to Jerusalem, *"Thy father was an Amorite, and thy mother a Hittite"* (Ezek. 16:3). Which could not be literally true, because Abraham and Sarah actually sprang from Shem, and the Amorites and Hittites from Ham. But it is said of *false teachers* under the Gospel, as Jannes and Jambres withstood Moses, so do these also resist the truth; men of corrupt minds, reprobate concerning the faith" (II Timothy 3:8). Jannes and Jambres were magicians of Egypt, who hardened the heart of Pharaoh against the call of God, to let Israel go and serve Him according to His own institutions. And Sodom was never more set against purity, nor Egypt against liberty, than the world and its religions now are against the purity and liberty of the Gospel. For truth is fallen in the street, and equity cannot enter (Isaiah 59:14). The nations of the world will not allow *a form of godliness* to be buried from among them; but how are they set against the power thereof! For as the body without the spirit is dead, so faith without works is dead also (James 2:26). "*Thou hast a name that thou livest, and art dead*" (Rev. 3:1). Whereas an inspired apostle said, "*The law of the spirit of life in Christ Jesus, hath made me free from the law of sin and death*" (Romans 8:2). "*We having the same spirit of faith, according as it is written, I believed, and therefore have I spoken; we also believe, and therefore speak. . . . .For our light affliction, which is but for a moment, worketh for us a far more exceeding and eternal weight of glory; while we look not at the things which are seen, but at the things which are not seen; for the things which are seen, are temporal; but the things which are not seen are eternal*" (II Cor. 4:13-18). But how is this life of faith now killed by a deceitful world!

Though the prophecy says, "*After three days and a half, the Spirit of life from God entered into them; and they stood upon their feet, and great fear fell upon them which saw them. And they heard a great voice from heaven, saying unto them, Come up hither. And they ascended up to heaven in a cloud, and their enemies beheld them. And the same hour was there a great earthquake, and the tenth part of the city fell, and in the earthquake were slain of men seven thousand; and the remnant were affrighted, and gave glory to the God of heaven. The second woe is past, and behold, the third woe cometh quickly. And the seventh angel sounded, and there were great voices in heaven, saying, 'The kingdoms of this world are become the kingdoms of our Lord, and of His Christ, and He shall reign forever and ever*" (Rev. 11:11-15). And we are to observe, that when the seventh angel shall begin to sound his trumpet, the mystery of God shall be finished, as He hath declared by all His prophets. (Rev. 10:7). The resurrection of the two witnesses in the eleventh chapter and the resurrection of the souls of the faithful in the twentieth chapter, appear to be the same glorious event, given under different views. For our Lord said to John, "*Write the things which thou hast seen, and the things which are, and the things which shall be hereafter*" (Rev. 1:19). When Christ was born of a virgin, in the true church of God, the nation of Israel was part of the Roman Empire, which had seven heads, and ten horns; and Herod sought to slay the child Jesus, as soon as He was born, and Pilate crucified Him, after which He was caught up unto God, and to His throne, where He will rule all nations with a rod of iron, and dash them in pieces like a potter's vessel. (Rev. 12:1-5; Luke 1:32,33) Matt. 2:3; 27:24; Acts 2:23-24; 4:25-28; and Psalm 2:1-9). And these things John *had seen.* He had seen the crucifying of Christ by the rulers of the Roman Empire, urged on to do it by false teachers among the Jews; for God had before said, "*The ancient and honorable, he is the head; and the prophet that teacheth, he is the tail*" (Isaiah 9:15). And deceitful teachers have ever been the meanest and worst of all men upon earth, and they were the tail of the dragon in the Roman Empire. But no men who have supposed that this twelfth chapter speaks of another child who should be born after the Apostolic Age, could ever give any rational account of him. Many have supposed it was Constantine, the first emperor who owned the so-called "Christian" name; but he divided the empire, and prepared the way for the advancement of the Man of Sin, as we have before proved. And after the ascension of Christ to heaven, it was said, "*Now is come salvation and strength, and the kingdom of our God, and the power of His Christ; for the Accuser of our brethren is cast down, which accused them before our God day and night. And they overcame him by the blood of the Lamb, and by the word of their testimony; and they loved not their lives unto the death*" (Rev. 12:10,11). In this way the power of the Devil was destroyed in the old Roman Empire. And when Satan shall be bound, so as not to deceive the nations any more, the prophecy says, "*I say thrones, and they sat upon them, and judgment was given unto them; and I saw the souls of them that were beheaded for the witness of Jesus, and for the word of God, and which had not worshipped the beast, neither his image, neither had received his mark upon their foreheads, or in their hands; and they lived and reigned with Christ a thousand years, But the rest of the dead lived not again until the thousand years were finished. This is the first resurrection*" (Rev. 20:4,5). And is not this the same resurrection which is spoken of in the eleventh chapter? For the kingdoms of this world will become the kingdoms of our Lord, and of His Christ, according to each of these prophecies. Daniel says, "*The saints of the Most High shall take the kingdom, and possess the kingdom forever, even forever and ever*" (Daniel 7:18). And the raising of the souls of the old martyrs appears to mean the same as the coming of John in the spirit and power of Elijah (Mal.4:5-6; and Luke 1:17). Neither have we any more reason to think that the bodies of all the saints will be raised, before their reign with Christ a thousand years, than the Jews had to expect that Elijah would personally come down from heaven, before the Messiah appeared among them. As all men are dead in trespasses and sins, until they are made alive to God, through Jesus Christ our Lord, and yet they have ever assumed the place of lawgivers and judges for the church of Christ, I believe that when God says, "*The rest of the dead lived not again until the thousand years were finished,*" He means that they shall not have the power of government over the church, as they have ever had since the rise of antichrist. For as Christ is the only Husband of His Bride, the church, how much like Sodom are all men who assume any power of government over her in religious affairs, so as to hinder her from obeying Him as a chaste virgin! There were some ministers of the devil, who transformed themselves as the ministers of righteousness, in the Apostolic Age, whose end was according to their works (II Cor. 11:2-15). And we may well conclude that there are many such in our day; and how pernicious in their influence among all people who receive them! And supporting such with the sword, is using of it to uphold the kingdom of the devil! "*Nevertheless, the foundation of God standeth sure, having this seal, The Lord knoweth them that are His. And let every one that nameth the name of Christ, depart from iniquity.*"

We readily grant that no prophecy of Scripture was ever clearly understood by men, until the event explained it. The disciples of Christ knew not the Scriptures that He was to rise again from he dead, until He appeared to them and explained the prophecies concerning it. (Luke 24:25-27 and John 20:9). And how long was it before they were clearly convinced that circumcision was abolished? And it is most evident that all National Churches have sprung from an abuse of the covenant of circumcision. That covenant gave Israel a right to seize upon the lands of the heathen in Canaan, and to buy others for servants; and all the plantations that have been made in America, under the name of "Christianity," have been made by those who imagined that "Christians" had a right to deal thus with all heathens. But as our Lord hath expressly excluded slavery, and the use of the sword of the magistrate from the government of His church, we may know that all these things belong to Mystery Babylon, the false "church." Literal Babylon had her name from Babel, where they said, *"Let us build us a city and a tower whose top may reach unto heaven, and let us make us a name, lest we be scattered abroad upon the face of all the earth* (Genesis 11:4). Is not the pursuit of all men naturally, to get to heaven by their own doings, and to make themselves a name upon the earth? Babel signifies *confusion;* and an inspired apostle says, *"Where envying and strife is, there is **confusion,** and every evil work. But the wisdom that is from above, is first pure, then peaceable, gentle, and easy to be entreated, full of mercy and good fruits, without partiality and without hypocrisy"* (James 3:16-17). And no men have this wisdom, but they who are born again by the Spirit of God. And to such another apostle says, "We have not followed cunningly devised fables, when we made known unto you the power and coming of our Lord Jesus Christ, but were eye-witnesses of His majesty. For he received from God the Father, honor and glory, when there came such a voice to Him from the excellent glory, This is My beloved Son, in whom I am well pleased. And this voice which came from heaven we heard, when we were with Him in the mount. We have also a more sure word of prophecy, whereunto ye do well that ye take heed, as unto a light that shineth in a dark place, until the day dawn, and the day-star arise in your hearts; knowing this first, that no prophecy of the Scripture is of any private interpretation. For the prophecy came not in old time by the will of man; but by holy men of God spoke as they were moved by the Holy Ghost. But there were false prophets also among the people, even as there shall be false teachers among you, who privily shall bring in damnable heresies, even denying the Lord that bought them, and bring upon themselves swift destruction. And many shall follow their pernicious ways, by reason of whom the way of truth shall be evil spoken of. And through covetousness, shall they with feigned words make merchandise of you; whose judgment now of a long time lingereth not, and their damnation slumbereth not" (II Peter 1:16-21; 2:1-3). How clearly are our times here described! For the fleets and armies which have filled the world with confusion and slavery, have been raised and upheld by national churches; and their vast funds of money, which are daily bought and sold by deceitful men to enrich themselves, have been kept in credit by the labors of the faithful. Thus, God says, "shall they make merchandise of you." And if it had not been for this wicked conduct our national debt might all have been paid off before now. But instead of it the debt is daily increasing, and many have tried all their arts to draw America into another war with foreign nations. Though when the church of Christ shall be wholly governed by His laws, above all the powers of the world, nation shall not lift up sword against nation, neither shall they learn war any more. (Isaiah 2:1-4).

But, instead of such a blessing, more blood has been shed in latter ages, by the nations who have borne the name of "Christianity," than by all other nations in the world; and this is now loudly proclaimed in Europe and America, as a strong argument against divine revelation. We have just seen that damnable heresies will cause the way of truth to be evil spoken of. The light of revelation has ever enlarged the capacities of men, beyond any other means in the world; but they who have not received the word into an honest and good heart, have been hardened afterwards like a rock, or have been as sharp as thorns, to tear away the property, or to destroy the lives of others (Luke 8:4-15). But that which beareth thorns and briers is rejected, and is nigh unto cursing, whose end is to be burned (Heb. 6:8). Yet many teachers now bring this last passage, to prove that the true children of God may fall away and perish forever' while others are holding up hell as a purging fire, which will finally purge away all sin from every child of Adam (universalism): as if the sufferings of a creature could purge away sin, instead of the blood of Christ applied by the Spirit of God. Thus they crucify to themselves the Son of God afresh, and put Him to an open shame. His person was crucified between two thieves, and His cause is crucified between opposite teachers and professors. But our Lord says, *"Enter ye in at the strait gate; for wide is the gate, and broad is the way, that leadeth to destruction, and many there be who go in thereat; because strait is the gate, and narrow is the way, which leadeth unto life, and few there be that find it"* (Matt. 7:13,14). Though the world is full of men who deny this, and who bring in damnable heresies. And they have perverted this word so much, as often to turn it against all those who have withdrawn from worldly churches, while others have applied the word to doctrines rather than practice. But if we take our ideas from the word of God, and not from the traditions of men, we may find that heresy means *rebellion* against God in His church. For when the Jews accused Paul of sedition, and being a leader of a new sect, he denied the charge, and said, *"After the way which they call heresy, so worship I the God of my fathers, believing all things which are written in the law and the prophets"* (Acts 24:5-14). They accused him of rebellion against government, and of being the leader of a new sect, who preferred Jesus of Nazareth above Moses, the great lawgiver to Israel. This last charge he owns, and so was a firm believer in revelation, while they rejected the counsel of God against themselves. And each heretic is subverted, and sinneth, being condemned of himself. (Titus 3:10-11). For our Lord says, *"All things whatsoever ye would that men should do to you, do ye even so to them; for this is the law and the prophets."* And each professor who breaks this law of equity, and will not repent, is to be rejected by the church. And when such men form other communities (religious societies), with other laws than the laws of Christ, it is a way which tries the hearts of all. Therefore the voice of inspiration says, *"If any man seem to be contentious, we have no such custom, neither the churches of God. Now in this that I declare unto you, I praise you not, that you come together not for the better, but for the worse. For first of all, when ye come together in the church, I hear that there be divisions among you, and I partly believe it. For there must also be heresies among you, that they which are approved may be made manifest among you.* (I Cor. 11:16-19). Hatred, variance, emulations, wrath, strife, seditions and heresies, are all works of the flesh. (Galatians 5:20). Now in all these passages, heresy appears to mean rebellion against God in His church. And another apostle says of them who loved the world above God, *"They went out from us; but they were not of us; for if they had been of us, they would no doubt have continued with us; but they went out, that they might be made manifest, that they were not all of us. And this is the spirit of antichrist"* (I John 15-19). All religious communities wherein the love of the world prevails above the love of God, are chargeable with "damnable heresies."

In monarchical governments the power is in a few hands, but in America all power of government is derived from the people, who have a fair opportunity to know teachers by their fruits. And where is the man who cannot distinguish thorns and brambles from trees which bear good fruit? (Luke 6: 44,45). Our Lord here plainly refers us to a parable concerning the first man who set himself up as king of the church of Israel, when God was their only king. All the good trees refused any such power over other trees, but the bramble said, "If in truth ye anoint me king over you, then come and put your trust in my shadow; and if not, let fire come out of the bramble, and devour the cedars of Lebanon" (Judges 9:8-15). *"The tongue sitteth on fire the course of nature, and it is set on fire of hell."* (James 3:6). And such men would destroy the best characters in the land, if they would not yield to their darling schemes. But no man should ever be elected into office, who has not been found to be a good tree by his fruits in private stations; and all teachers should be avoided, as wolves in sheep's clothing, who tear away the property of any unjustly. And it is impossible for any community to be clear of this evil, where religious teachers are supported by force. For as the church of Israel were never allowed to do it, when they came into that practice, God said, "Her *princes within her are roaring lions, her judges are evening wolves, they gnaw out the bones till the morrow. Her prophets are light and treacherous persons, her priests have polluted the sanctuary, they have done violence to the law"* (Zeph. 3:3,4). And all the natural lions and wolves in the world, never destroyed so many men, as National Churches have done in our day. Again it was said of Israel, *"The heads thereof judge for **reward**, and the priests thereof teach **for hire,** and the prophets thereof **divine for money**; yet will they lean upon the Lord, and say, 'Is not the Lord among us? None evil can come upon us. But for these iniquities their nation was ruined, and the mountain of the house of God will be exalted above all earthly powers, when wars shall come to an end."* (Micah 3:11-12; 4:1-5). Is not the Lord among us? None evil can come upon us, was the language which brought ruin upon Jerusalem, and such confidence in negatives will ruin all people who build thereon. For reason as well as Scripture discovers that the more light men have, the greater is their guilt and misery when they sin against it. But when the knowledge of the Lord shall cover the earth as the waters cover the sea, the wolf shall dwell with the lamb, and they shall not hurt nor destroy in all His holy mountain. (Isaiah 11:6-9). And this is life eternal, that they might know Thee the only true God, and Jesus Christ whom Thou hast sent. (John 17:3). This is the only way of peace and eternal happiness.

The End

We credit, with thankfulness, Mr. George Howgego in England for the discovery of the book "Sovereign Grace" by Isaac Backus, and his loan of that book for republication, and also Hoyt Sparks of North Carolina for scanning and correcting the materials for us.

www.ingramcontent.com/pod-product-compliance
Lightning Source LLC
Chambersburg PA
CBHW081150090426
42736CB00017B/3263